THE VERSES
OF
VEMANA

THE VERSES
OF
VEMANA

MORAL, RELIGIOUS, AND SATIRICAL

Translated

RV CHARLES PHILIP BROWN
OF THE MADRAS CIVIL SERVICE

GYAN

Published by

GYAN

Gyan Publishing House
5, Ansari Road
Daryaganj, New Delhi-110002
Phone: 011-47034999, 9811692060
E-mail: books@gyanbooks.com

Distribution Network
gyanbooks.com
India, USA, Canada, UK, Australia, France

ISBN : 978-81-212-4183-0 (PB)
First Published, 1911

2nd Impression 2020

Printed at: Gyan Press, Delhi.

The Verses of Vemana
Translated by: Rv Charles Philip Brown

వేమనపద్యములు.

THE VERSES

OF

VÈMANA

MORAL, RELIGIOUS, AND SATIRICAL

Translated

By CHARLES PHILIP BROWN

OF THE MADRAS CIVIL SERVICE

MADRAS :

V. RAMASWAMY SASTRULU & SONS

1911.

పద్యకావ్యములు

		ప్రతి 1-కి రూ.	అ.
అవనిముత్తెలు	...	0	8
ఆధ్యాత్మరామాయణము	...	2	0
అనంతునిఛందము, (ఛందోదర్పణము)	...	2	0
అనిరుద్ధచరిత్రము	...	1	0
కవిత్వతత్త్వవిచారవిమర్శనము	...	1	8
అంబరీషోపాఖ్యానము, సటీక	...	0	6
ఆముక్తమాల్యద, (విష్ణుచిత్తీయము)	...	6	0
ఆంజనేయదండకము, హనుమద్దండకము	...	0	4
ఆంధ్రభాగవతము, పద్యకావ్యము, 2 సంపుటములు	...	15	0
ఆదిపర్వము, పద్యకావ్యము, [illegible]	...	1	8
,, టీక	...	4	0
ఆంధ్రభారతము, పద్యకావ్యము:—			
ఆది సభాపర్వములు కలసంపుటము	...	4	0
అరణ్యపర్వము	...	4	0
విరాటోద్యోగపర్వములు	...	4	0
భీష్మద్రోణపర్వములు	...	4	0
కర్ణశల్యసౌప్తిక స్త్రీపర్వములు	...	4	0
శాంతిపర్వము	...	4	0
అనుశాసనిక, అశ్వమేధ, ఆశ్రమవాస, మౌసల, మహాప్రస్థానిక, స్వర్గారోహణపర్వములు	...	4	0
ఆదిపంచకము, ఒకటేసంపుటము	...	11	4
యుద్ధపంచకము, స్త్రీపర్వము	...	7	8
శాంతిసప్తకము	...	7	8
ఆంధ్రభారతవిమర్శనము, మల్లాది సూర్యనారాయణశాస్త్రి గారిది		0	12

Audi Saraswaty Nilaya Press,
Tandaiyarpet, Madras.

PREFACE

WHEN commencing the study of a language, we are naturally led to enquire for works popular among the natives themselves, but composed in a style easy enough to be comprehended without difficulty by a foreigner. Such an enquiry in the year 1824 regarding Telugu made me acquainted with the verses collected in the present volume. Several manuscripts of VEMA, or VEMANA, (for both names are used) were put into my hands, which I perused and translated in such hours of leisure as my public employments allowed. They proved to be full of errors of every kind, in orthography, metre, and meaning ; no two copies followed the same arrangement, and they varied in extent from two to eight hundred epigrams. After collecting such copies as were to be found at Masulipatam where I was then stationed, I gradually procured others from Vizagapatam, Nellore, Guntoor, Cuddapah, and Madras. I then caused an index to be drawn up wherein nine columns exhibited the places at which the verses appeared in as many manuscripts, which I thus was enabled to collate. The number of stanzas I found amounted to about 2,500 ; a comparison, however, showed that the total was little more than 2000.

It next became necessary to reduce the verses to some regular arrangement. Each transcriber had evidently selected such as he preferred, and no order was any where preserved. I at length formed the whole into five tolerably consistent divisions—religious, moral, satirical, mystic, and miscellaneous. The two last of these form more than half the work, but are omitted in the present volume because devoid of interest and utility. The student will perhaps find the second and third chapters easier than the first, which may, therefore, be read afterwards.

A system of obscure and unprofitable doctrines regarding mysticism is much studied among the Telugus ; in such reveries VEMANA has indulged at great length, and there his meaning is often doubtful. Of such verses I have retained only a few of the easiest. Among the satirical epigrams I have omitted several wherein railing was substituted for just remarks; and should perhaps have excluded yet more, but that I observed these to be remarkably popular among the Telugus.

A few others are left out as more properly belonging to the collections known by the names of BHASCARA and SUMATI, while some were rejected as being riddles attributed not to *Vemana* but an epigrammatist named TIRUMALESA.

A miscellaneous collection of unconnected verses like the present, is generally denominated a *satacam*, which answers to the *Garlands* or *Centuries* composed by English poets in old days, being a series of verses which are similar in metre, subject, and chorus. These are generally numbered in seperate hundreds, but it appeared unnecessary to retain either that arrangement, or that title, in the present volume, which more nearly resembles the Anthologies collected in Greek and Latin literature.

It is not easy to ascertain any thing regarding the history of Vemana, which is the personal name of the author, and sometimes occurs, though rarely, among the Telugus of the present day. His family name he never discloses, and I hence imagine him to have been a *Zangam*: the sect of *Sudras* known by this name are seceders from the *common religion*; they worship Siva alone, and, on embracing the Zangam sect, they give up their family appellation, and are then usually called by the name of the sect alone. Their creed also corresponds with that taught by Vemana, and this is the only one not satirized by him.

Of his birth-place and circumstances very slight traditions have been preserved. He was by birth a *capu* or farmer. Some assert that he belonged to the family of Ana Vema Reddi, a chief in the candanul (or Curnool) country; and the brother of the poet is said to have commanded the fort of Gandicota. Some believe him to have been a native of Crishtipad in Candanul: others, of Inaconda in Guntoor: and I have also heard it said that he was born at Chitwel in Cuddappah district; but I have had opportunities of inquiring at all these places and have, after all, gained no information whatever. Yet his dialect in a few passages renders it probable that Vemana was a native of the south-western parts of Telingana, where these towns are situated: and it is believed that he lived about the beginning of the seventeenth century of our era.

This author is in Telugu literature what Lucian is in Greek—a familiar writer, useful to a beginner, though neither poetical nor classical. Very different indeed from the numerous refined compositions that adorn the language, yet far more profitable to those who do not as yet attempt higher branches of reading. The terse and condensed style used in the proverbs and maxims of all languages cannot be expected to exemplify every form of the verb or every intricacy of syntax. For these the reader must resort to compositions more polished and more deversified.

NOTE.

Most of the verses in this author are, like the first twenty, composed in the Ataveladi metre, and have one uniform chorus;

Viswad abhi rama vinara Vema,

the first syllable ot which, (వి.) placed at the end of such verses denotes the repetition. For "Viswad abhi" some copies have viswat abhi," and others "viswat obhi." The import of the chorus is obscure, but the sense of each verse is complete without it. Some believe that the "Vema" so addressed was the elder brother of the moralist.

The notes and the indexes will, I hope, furnish every information required by the reader.

VARIOUS READINGS.

I. 20 line 3, నెట్టివారికై'న పుట్టవో యాశలు?

II. 101 line 1, యుబుసు పోవకనై'న.

Most of the manuscripts of this author commence with one of the following verses, which belong rather to the mystic chapter.

క. శివ కవులకు నవ కవులకు,
శివ భక్తికి తత్వ మునకు, చింతామణికిన్,
శివ లోక ప్రమథులకును,
శివునకు గురువునకు శరణు సేయర వేమా.

తే. శ్రీకరంబుగ వేమన జెప్పి నట్టి
పద్యముల నెవ్వడే నియు పఠన సేయు
న'ట్టి పురుషుడు, మన మునని' ట్టిద' నుచు
జెప్పరా న ట్టి వస్తువు జేరు వేమ.

To the auspicious Bards, to the Nine Poets, to the Siva creed, to his Essence, to the boon-granting gem, to those who attend in the presense of Siva, to the God himself, and to thy teacher— pray for aid, O Vema!

Whoever shall study the verses composed by the propitious Vemana, that man shall attain to That Object which is in its nature indescribable.

వేమనపద్యములు

ప్రథమ భాగము.

వేమన' నగ యోగి వెలసె లోకములోన;
పూజలి' డుడు, పుణ్య - పురుషులార;
పూజలి' డిన యంత, భుక్తి ముక్తుల ని' చ్చు
విశ్వదాభిరామ వినర వేమ. ౧

పలుకుమ' న్న నే' ల పలుకక యున్నావు;
పలుకుమ' య్య, నాతో ప్రబలముగను;
పలుకుమ' య్య ! నీదు పలుకు నేనె' రిగెద. వి. ౨

THE VERSES OF VEMANA

TRANSLATION.

BOOK I.

1. The Yogi named Vemana hath shone forth in the world ; bow to him, ye men of virtue! while ye reverence him he will bestow on you sustenance and perfection. Listen, O Vema, dear to the Lord of all!

2. When I cry "Speak, O God," why speakest thou not? O speak to me, and powerfully! Speak, O father, surely I shall recognize thy voice!

ఆత్మ - శుద్ధి లేని యాచారమ' ది యేల ?
భాండ - శుద్ధి లేని పాకమే' ల ?
చిత్త - శుద్ధి లేని శివ పూజలే' లరా? వి. ౩

నిక్కమై' న మంచి నీలమొ' క్కటి చాలు ;
తళుకు బెళుకు రాళ్లు తట్టెడే' ల ?
చదువ పద్యమ' రయ జాలదా' యొక్కటి ? వి. ౪

నిన్ను జూచెనే' ని తన్ను తా మరచును ;
తన్ను జూచెనే' ని నిన్ను మరచు ;
నే' విధమున జనుడు నెరుగు, నిన్నును దన్ను ? వి. ౫.

మురియు వాడె' వండు ? మురియని దె' వ్వండు ?
పాటు జేసి చూడ' బట్ట బయలు ;
సారది జల - ఘటమున సూర్యుని - చందంబు. వి. ౬

---

3. Observances void of purity of heart! to what end are they? to what end is the preparation of food without cleansing the vessel? void of purity of mind, to what end is the worship of God?

4. One real and good sapphire is enough, why collect a basketful of glittering, sparkling stones? *consider then*, is not one verse, if worth reading, sufficient?

5. While he looks to thee, O God, he forgets thee. How shall a man learn to know himself and thee?

6. Who is the joyful man? who is the unhappy? if thou seek to know this, this is as evident as the sun shining down into a vessel of water.

గాజు కుప్పె లోన కడగుచు దీపంబు
యెట్టులు' ండు, జ్ఞానమ' ట్టులు' ండు
తెలిసిన' ట్టి వారి దేహంబుల' ందుల. వి. ౭

కల్ల - గురుడు గట్టు, నె' ల్ల కర్మంబుల ;
మధ్య - గురుడు గట్టు, మంత్ర - చయము ;
ఉత్తముండు కట్టు, యోగ - సామ్రాజ్యంబు. వి.

పెట్టి పొయ్య లేని వట్టి నరులు భూమి ;
పుట్టనే' మి ? వారు గిట్ట నేమి ?
పుట్టలోన చెదలు పుట్టదా గిట్టదా ? వి.

తాము గన్న - వారు తము గన్న - వారును
చచ్చు టె' ల్ల, తమకు సాక్షి గాదె ?
బ్రతుకు టె' ల్ల తమకు బ్రహ్మ - కల్పంబులా? వి. ౧౦

---

7. Even as a lamp shines in a glass vase, thus shineth wisdom dwelling in the bodies of men of understanding.

8. A false teacher restrains us in all our acts. The middling, ordinary teacher makes a multitude of senseless spells. But the good one combines the whole power of excellence.

9. Profitless are those men who will bestow neither meat nor drink: what though they be born in the world? what though they die? are not the white-ants of the hillock also born? and do they not die also?

10. Is not the dying of all those we bring forth and of those who bring us forth, an evidence to us? Shall our life be to us as the eternity of God?

ఎరుక మాలు వాడు యేమే' మి చదివిన ;
చదివిన' ంత సేపు సద్గుణి యగు ;
కదసి తామరందు కప్ప గూర్చున్నట్లు. వి. ౧౧

కూటికినె' డ బాసి కూర్చిన మనుజుఁడు ;
వెలదుల గనుగొన్న వెతల జిక్కు ;
చెలగి యగ్ని చూచు శలభంబు చాడ్పున. వి. ౧౨

కసువు బసికిఁ జేసె, గాలి ఫణికి జేసె ;
మన్నె ' రలకు జేసె, మరవ కె' ట్లు ;
కుంభిని బసులకును కూడ' ట్లు చేసెరా ? వి. ౧౩

ఎవ్వరి గుణములును యేమ' న్న మానవు ;
చక్క జేయ రాదు, కుక్కతోక ;
గడుసురాలు మగని గంప బెట్ట' మ్మురా. వి. ౧౪

11. Whatever he may read who is devoid of understanding, his virtue continues only so long as he is reading ; even as a frog *is dignifiied only so long as it* is seated on a lotus leaf.

12. At the sight of women the cupidinous man quits his meal, being stricken with the pain *of desire* ; even as the grasshopper delights in viewing the fire *that will destory it.*

13. Grass he created for cattle : wind as food for the serpent : and earth for the earth-worm, forgetting none : behold how he hath prepared food for all the inhabitants of the globe !

14. No man's disposition will alter, say what we may ; neither can a dog's tail be made straight : the stubborn woman will even put her husband in a basket *and* sell him.

వేరు - పురుగు చేరి, వృక్షంబుఁ జెరుచును ;
చీడ - పురుగు చేరి, చెట్టుఁ జెరుచు ;
కుత్సితుండు చేరి, గుణవంతుఁ జెరుచురా. వి. ౧౫

ఉప్పు కప్పురంబు నొక్క పోలికెనుండు ;
చూడఁ జూడ రుచుల జాడ వేరు ;
పురుషులందు పుణ్య - పురుషులు వేరయా. వి. ౧౬

జీవి పోక ముందె జీవ - వస్తువులిచ్చి,
జీవి నిలుప వలయు జీవనముగ ;
జీవి తొలఁగు వెనక జీవ - వస్తువులేల ? వి. ౧౭

కల్ల నిజము రెండు కర - కంఠుఁడెరుగును ,
నీరు పల్లమెరుగు, నిజముగాను :
తనయుని జననంబు తల్లిఁదానెరుగును. వి. ౧౮

15. The root-worm destroys the tree ; the sap-worm destroys the herb ; and the backbiter ruins every good quality.

16. Salt and camphor are of one semblance ; but if you examine and try the flavors, their tastes are diverse : thus do the excellent differ *from other men*.

17. Before the spirit depart give vital medicines and stay the soul in life ; but when the soul hath departed, to what end are reviving remedies ?

18. Truth and falsehood the Great Spirit alone knows : water alone truly knows the declivity and the rising ground : and the mother alone knows the generation of her son *and who is his father*.

అంగమె' ల్ల వడలి, యటు దంతములు నూ' డి,
తనువు ముదిమిచేత దరుచు వడక ;
ముప్పు - తిప్పల బడి మోహంబు విడువడు. వి. ౧౯

ఆడు వారి గన్న న' ర్థంబు పొడ గన్న ;
సారమై' న రుచుల చవులు గన్న ;
యయ్యగాండ్లకై' ననా' శలు బుట్టవా ? వి. ౨౦

అనువు గాని చోటన' ధికులమ' నరాదు ;
కొంచెము' ండుటె' ల్ల కొదువ గాదు ;
కొండ యద్దమందు కొంచమై' యుండదా ? వి. ౨౧

తన - మది కపటము గలిగిన ;
తనవలెనే కపటము' ండు, తగ జీవులకున్
తన - మది కపటము విడిచిన ;
తనకె' వ్వడు కపటి లేడు, ధరలో వేమా ! ౨౨

---

19. Though the limbs all wither, the teeth drop out, and the body tremble greatly with decrepitude ; though they be infirm with age, cupidity will never leave man.

20. If they see women, view wealth, or taste delicious sweets, will not desires be produced in all, even the best of men ?

21. In an unsuitable place never let us hold ourselves superior. To be low is no humiliation. Small is the image of a hill in a mirror.

22. If thine own mind contain duplicity, others will, like thyself, use craft towards thee : but if dissimulation leave thy heart, none in the world will be deceitful toward thee.

చంప దగిన యట్టి శత్రుడు తన - చేత
జిక్కె-నే' ని, కీడు సేయ రాదు.
పొసగ మేలు జేసి పొమ్మ' నుటే' చావు! వి. ౨౩

తామసించి సేయ తగదె' ట్టికార్యంబు:
వేగిరింపన' దియు విషమము' గును -
పచ్చి-కాయ దెచ్చి' పడ-వేయ' ఫలమా' నె? వి. ౨౪

నీళ్ల లోన నోడ నిగిడి తిన్నగ బ్రాకు;
బైట మూరెడై' న బ్రాక లేదు:
నెలవు దప్పు చోట నేర్పరి కొర గాదు! వి. ౨౫

నీళ్ల లోన మొసలి నిగిడి యేనుగు బట్టు;
బైట కుక్క చేత భంగ పడును;
స్థాన-బలిమి గాని' తన - బల్మి కాద' యా; వి. ౨౬

---

23. Though a foe worthy of death fall into thy hand, afflict him not: Conciliate him by goodness and bid him depart. This is death to him!

24. It is fit to perform no act tardily; if thou hurry it, it will itself become evil. If thou take and cast down a raw fruit, will it ripen?

25. In the waters a ship will float and swim smoothly: but if out, it cannot crawl even a cubit. Thus where he is not at home, the skilful is of no avail.

26. A crocodile while swimming in water will seize *and destroy* an elephant; but out *of the stream* it is discomfited *even* by a dog. Its might *then* is local, not individual.

కులము లో నొకండు గుణవంతుఁ డుండెనా ?
కులము వెలయు, వాని గుణముచేత.
వెలయు వనము లోన మలయ-జంబు న్నట్లు. వి. ౨౭

పంది పిల్ల లీను, పదియు నైదింటిని ;
కుంజరంబు యీను, కొదమ నొకటి.
యుత్తమ - పురుషుండు యొక్కఁడు జాలఁడా? వి. ౨౮

ఎరుఁగు వాని దెలుప నెవ్వఁడైనను జాలు ;
నొరుల వశము గాదు వోగు దెల్ప ;
యేటి వంక దీర్ప నెవ్వరి తరమయా ? వి. ౨౯

అల్పుఁ డెపుడు బల్కు నాడంబరము గాను,
సజ్జనుండు బలుకు, చల్ల గాను.
కంచు మోగిన ట్లు కనకంబు మోగునా? వి. ౩౦

---

27. If there be in a tribe one of excellence, the tribe becomes illustrious by reason of his virtues, as the grove is distinguished for the sandal tree therein.

28. A pig will bring forth young at five or ten at a time: an elephant produces but one. Is not then one man truly excellent, enough ?

29. Any one can instruct a man of understanding, but it is not in the power of others to teach the vile: Is it possible for any one to straighten the bend of a river ?

30. The light man will always talk big, but the excellent speaks coolly. *Consider*, will gold ring like bell metal ?

ఓగు నో' గు మెచ్చు నో' నరంగన' జ్ఞాని
భావమి' చ్చ, మెచ్చు పరమ లుబ్ధు :
పంది బురద మెచ్చు, పన్నీరు మెచ్చునా ? వి. ౩౧
గంగ పారుచు' ండు, కదలని గతి తోడ ;
ముఱికి పారుచు' ండు, మ్రోఁత తోడ ;
దాతయోర్చిన' ట్ల ధముడో' ర్వఁగా లేడు. వి. ౩౨
కాని - వాని చేత కాసు వీసములి' చ్చి
వెంట ఁదిరుగు టె' ల్ల వెర్రితనము :
పిల్లి బట్ట కోడి పిలిచిన పలుకునా ? వి. ౩౩
పిసిని - వాని యింట పీనుగు వెడలిన,
కట్ట - కోలలకును కాసులి' చ్చి ;
వెచ్చమా' యెన' ంచు వెక్కి - వెక్కి డ్చురా. వి. ౩౪

---

31. The vile countenances (or applauds) the vile, and agreeably to this does the hard miser laud the mind of the fools : the swine delights in mud, will it take pleasure in rose water?

32. The Ganges flows with a tranquil course, but a foul *stream* rushes with a roar. Thus the base can never be mild as the noble.

33. If you have given your money* to an evil man to follow him about is all folly. If a cat has seized a fowl will it answer to your call?

34. If a corpse leave a miser's house when he has given the money for the shroud and bier, "alas for the fees!" cries he, sobbing and sobbing as he weeps!

---

* Literally, pence and farthings.

కష్ట - లోభి వాని కలిమికినా' సించి,
బడుగు - వాడు దిరుగు పరిణమించు ;
తగరు వెంట నక్క దగిలిన చందంబు. వి. ౩౫

లోభి - వాని ఁజంప లోకంబు లోపల
మందు వలదు ; వేరె మతము గలదు :
పైకమ' డుగ, చాల భగ్గున పడి చచ్చు. వి. ౩౬

మాటలె' ల్ల కల్ల, మనసె' ల్ల దొంగర్క-
మే; ' టి ప్రాణమి ?' ఁకనే' టి బ్రతుకు ?
మాట సత్యమై - తె మరి శతా - యుష్యంబు. వి. ౩౭

కలిమి నాడు నరుడు కానడు మదమున ;
లేమి నాడు మొదలె లేదు పెట్ట :
కలిమి లేమి లేని కాలంబు గలుగునా ? వి. ౩౮

---

35. Coveting the gains of the hard miser the poor man follows him and bends *humbly* : this attachment is like that of the fox to the ram.

36. Would you kill a miser: no poison in the world is requisite : there is another mode ; ask him for a penny, and he will instantly fall down dead.

37. All *their* words are a lie, *their* whole heart is set on fraud. To what end then is the soul any longer ? of what good is life ? If *thy* word be truth, this is a hundred additional years of life.

38. In the day of wealth a man is puffed up, and cannot see others ; when in poverty, he has nothing left to bestow: Is there any season free from *the ills both* of riches and those of poverty ?

కనియు గాన లేదు కదలింపడా నోరు;
వినియు వినఁగ లేదు విస్మయమున;
సంపద గల వాఁడు సన్నిపాతకమది. వి. ౩౯

తీర్పనోర్వ లేని తీర్పరి-తనమేల?
కూర్ప విప్ప లేప నేర్పరేల?
పెట్టి పొయ్య లేని వట్టి బీరములేల? వి. ౪౦

తాను గుడువ లేక, తగవాది యాప్తుల
జేరనీవ్వడ, ట్టి చెనటిగొడ్డు;
చేని లోన బొమ్మ జేసి కట్టిన యట్లు. వి. ౪౧

పూర్వ-జన్మమందు పుణ్యంబు సేయని
పాపి ధనము కాశ పడుట యెల్ల
విత్త మరచి కోయ వెదకిన చందంబు. వి. ౪౨

---

39. Seeing he cannot see, he will not open that mouth *of his*. Hearing heareth not, through arrogance. Such is the disorder * of the man of wealth!

40. To what end is an authority that can neither decide nor determine? of what use is a genius who neither can join nor loose? What good is there in *the* empty bragging *of those who* give neither meat nor drink?

41. He who neither eats for himself, nor will let his friends approach, the vicious brute, is like to a *lifeless* image (scarecrow) made and set up in a field.

42. If a sinner in his former birth performed no virtue, all his longing for wealth is like seeking to reap when you have forgotton to sow.

---

* Sannipat, nearly answering to *cachexia*, is a term applied to many diseases arising from no definite cause and admitting no specific remedy.

చమురు గలుగు దివ్వె సరవితో మండును,
చమురు లేని దివ్వె సమసి పోవు;
తనువు తీరనే'ని తలపు తోడనె తీరు. వి. ౪౩

భూపతి-కృప నమ్మి భూమి జెరుచు వాడు,
ప్రజల యుసురు దాకి పడును పిదప;
యెగర వేయు బంతి యెందాక నిల్చురా. వి. ౪౪

పాపమ'నగ వేరె పరదేశమున లేదు
తనదు కర్మములను దగిలియుండు;
కర్మ-తంత్రి గాక, గనుకని యుంటొ'ప్పు. వి. ౪౫

నక్క-వినయములను నైగారములు బల్కి
కుడువకెల్ల-ధనము కూడ బెట్టు
కొక్కు-బోను-వాత కూడు చల్లిన రీతి. వి. ౪౬

---

43. A lamp, *if* supplied with oil, flames meetly: a light devoid of oil expires. *Thus* when the body ceases *to live our* thoughts perish with it.

44. He that, relying on the prince, ruins the land, the sorrows of the people shall reach him, and at last he shall fall. How long shall the bounding ball retain its elevation.

45. What is called sin does not pertain to any peculiar place; it is attached to (or mingled with) our own acts. It is better, then, to keep one's eyes open, than to be a *laborious* performer of *meritorious* works.

46. Practising the humility of a fox, and talking obsequiously, he heaps up all his wealth, and does not use it: thus is rice sprinkled at the mouth of a bandicoot trap.

వెళ్ళి వచ్చు నాడు మళ్ళి పోయే నాడు ;
వెంట రాదు, ధనము కొంట బోదు ;
తాను యేడ బోనో ధనమేడ బోవునో ? వి. ౪౭

పుట్టు - బిత్తలి వలె పోవు - బిత్తలి వలె ;
తిరుగు - బిత్తలి వలె, దేహి ధరణి
యున్న నాటి కైన నుపకారి గాలేడు. వి. ౪౮

కాశి బోదుననుచు గడకట్టగానేల ?
వాశి - తీర్థములను వగవనేల ?
దోషకారికెట్లు దొరుకురా యాకాశి వి. ౪౯

ఇనుము విరిగెనేని యినుమారు ముమ్మారు
కాచి యతక నేర్చు కమ్మరీడు ;
మనసు విరిగెనేని మరి యంట నేర్చునా? వి. ౫౦

---

47. When he departs *this life* his riches follows him not, neither when he returns *in another transmigration*; when he again dies he carries not his wealth with him: where does he go and where does his wealth go?

48. Naked was he born and naked does he depart. He that is in the body wanders the earth as though naked: Long as he live he cannot become a doer of good.

49. Why make projects, saying, I will go to Casi (Benares)? why long after the noble *holy* springs? How shall that Benares (heaven) be attained by the evil doer?

50. Though iron break twice or thrice, the smith knows how to heat and weld it. If the spirit break who shall restore it?

పరనారీ - దూరగుడై ;
పరధనములకాస పడక పరహితచారై ;
పరుల' లిగిన తాన' లుగక
పరులె' న్నగ బ్రతుకువాడు ప్రాజ్ఞుడు వేమా. ౫౧

అజ్ఞానమె శూద్రత్వము ;
సుజ్ఞానము బ్రహ్మమా' ట శ్రుతులను వినరా !
యజ్ఞానము' డిగి వాల్మికి
సుజ్ఞానపు - బ్రహ్మమొం' దె జూడర వేమా ! ౫౨

నీళ్లలోని - చేఁప నెరి మాంసమా' శకు
గాలముం' దు జిక్కి కూలిన' ట్లు
యాశ బుట్టి మనుజుడా' రీతి జెడిపోవు ; వి. ౫౩

---

51. He who keeps himself afar from another's wife; who desireth not another's wealth, but is benevolent; and though others be enraged, is not worth; and who lives in the esteem of others, is the wise Man.

52. Listen to the scriptures, that declare ignorance to be the servile (Sudra) state, and wisdom to be (Braminship) the priestly rank. Behold Valmiki the bard (who was once a highwayman) when his ignorance ceased, attained the Braminical rank.

53. Like as the fish in the waters, through desire of the delicious bait, is fixed on the hook and perishes: so a man if seized with desire is also ruined.

బొంది యెవరి సొమ్ము పోషింప పలుమారు !
ప్రాణ మెవరి సొమ్ము భక్తి సేయ !
ధనము యెవరి సొమ్ము! ధర్మమే తన సొమ్ము. వి. ౫౪
నార యన నవచ్చు, నమశివ యనవచ్చు ;
మేలు - వారి నమ్మి మెచ్చ వచ్చు ;
కొంగు - కాసు విడిచి గొబ్బున నీ రాదు. వి. ౫౫
మేడి - పండు జూడ మేలిమై యుండును ;
పొట్ట విచ్చి చూడ పురుగులుండు ;
బెరుకు వాని మదిని బింకమీలాగురా. వి. ౫౬
ఉసురు లేసి తిత్తి యిసుమంత వూదిన
పంచ - లోహములును భస్మమౌను ;
పెద్దలుసురుమంటె పెను మంటలేగవా? వి. ౫౭

---

54. Whose is the body that we should continually nourish it? whose is the soul that we should be devout to save it? whose is our wealth? virtue alone is ours!

55. He may ejaculate Nara! (Arjuna) or Namasiva! (a name of the deity), and we may, in seeing him, say, Good! Admirable! and laud *him*; but he is in no hurry to open his purse and bestow a farthing.

56. If you behold the fig (*ficus glomerata*) it is like pure gold; if you open its belly and look in, it is all worms. Such is the ostentation of a reserved man.

57. By the groaning of a buffalo hide bellows (in the world)* the five metals are calcined: when good men grieve, will not a great flame arise *to heaven*?

---

* The words యిల, ధాత్రిన్, మహిలో, or భూమి, are often used in this author to fill up the metre. So also the words మరి, వినరా, జూడర &c.

మందు దిన బోటు మానును ;
మందు దినగ జేయ పొలతి మహిలో వలచున్ ;
మందు దిన కుదురు రోగము ;
మందు దినం గలదు, పుష్టి మహిలో వేమా. ౫౮

తలను పాగ పైని తగు - పచ్చడము బొజ్జ
చెవుల పోగుల' రసి చేరున' ర్థి ;
శుద్ధ - పశువులౌ' ట బుద్ధిలో నె' రుగక. వి. ౫౯

స్త్రీల సుఖము జూచి చిత్తంబు నిలుకడ
సేయని మనుజుండు చెడు నిజంబు ;
యేటి - గట్టు - మానుకె' ప్పుడు చలనంబు? వి. ౬౦

---

58. If the medicine is taken the wound will be cured. There is also a medicine which, if thou give it to her, a woman will love thee : there is a medicine by which disease is cured : if thou take a certain medicine, it causes fatness.

59. When he beholds a turban on the head, a well fitting coat, a fair belly and rings in the ears, the beggar approaches him, little supposing what a mere brute *the miser* really is.

60. He who being given up to the pleasures of women, cannot exercise firmness of mind, verily shall be ruined. Like as a tree on the river bank is ever unstable.

కూలినాలి జేసి, గుల్లా పుపని జేసి;
తెచ్చి పెట్ట యాలు మెచ్చ నేర్చు;
లేమి - జిక్క - విభుని వేమారు దిట్టును. వి. ౬౧

ఇంద్రియ పరవశుడ' ధముం
డిం' ద్రియ పరవశుడు భక్తియెడ మధ్యము డౌ;
నింద్రియ జయుడు' త్తముడు జి
తేంద్రియ సమ్మతుడు విన మహేశుడు వేమా.

తన గుణము తనకును' డగ
నెనయంగా నొరుని - గుణము నెం' చును, మదిలో
తనగుణము తాను దెలియక,
పనరి యొరుని న' నెడు వాడు భ్రష్టుడు వేమా. ౬౩

61. If thou wilt work for hire, and slave, and gain, and give it to thy wife, she knows to applaud thee: but a thousand-fold will she revile her husband if he falls into poverty.

62. He that is given up to his senses is the lowest. He that is delivered up to his lusts shall through devotion become medial. He is the best who hath conquered his lusts. He who hath subdued his passions and commandeth himself is (hear me) the mighty lord!

63. His own disposition remaining *unaltered* in him he concerns himself to weigh in his mind the temper of another! He who, himself yet ignorant of his own nature laments only for his neighbour, is a fallen creature, O

వెర్రి - వానికైన వేష - ధారికైన,
రోగికైన పరమ - యోగికైన,
స్త్రీలఁ జూచినప్పుడు చిత్తంబు రంజిల్లు. వి. ౬౪

తావసించు - చోట తగనల్లడయెనా?
సౌఖ్యము గల భూమి జరుద వలయు;
కొలకులింకెనేని కొంగలందుండునా? వి. ౬౫

భూమిలోన పుణ్య - పురుషులు లేకున్న
జగములేల నిచ్చు పోగులు గాక
నంత తరుచు దొరకరాడనాడను గాని. వి. ౬౬

చిత్త - శుద్ధి గల్గి చేసిన పుణ్యంబు,
కొంచెమైననదియు కొదువ గాదు;
విత్తనంబు మఱ్ఱి - వృక్షంబునకునెంత. వి. ౬౭

---

64. Whether he be a fool or a fop, be he a patient or a pre-eminent ascetic, instantly on beholding women is the heart of a man delighted.

65. If the place where you are is troubled, you should pass to a more comfortable land. If the pond dry, will the cranes remain in it? (An allusion to a fable in the Hitopadesa.)

66. Were the earth void of the excellently virtuous, how should the world stand nor be burnt with *fire*? They are not so very frequent: but only here and there.

67. A good work performed with a pure heart, though small, is not trifling. How large is the seed of the banyan *and the mustard* tree!

చెడ్డ వాని మిగులఁ జెరుచును దైవంబు
అడ్డ పడడు వానికాపదైన;
చెడిన - చేనుఁ జూచి యొడయుడు మెచ్చునా? వి. ౬౮

ఎక్కుడైన - యాశలినుమడి యుండఁగా;
తిక్కబట్టి నరుడు తిరుగుచుండు;
కుక్కవంటి - యాశ కూర్చుండనివ్వదు. వి. ౬౯

అరయ తరుచు కల్లలాడెడు - వారిండ్ల
వెడలకేల లక్ష్మి విశ్రమించు?
ఓటి కుండ నీరు పోసిన చందాన. వి. * ౭౦

గుణవతి యగు యువతి గృహము చక్కగనుండు,
చీకటింట దివ్వె చెలగు రీతి;
దేవి యున్న యిల్లు దేవార్చన - గృహంబు. వి. ౭౧

---

68. Utterly does the Deity destory the wicked. God does not interpose if evil befall him. Will the king be pleased at seeing a barren field?

69. When his passions are redoubled, a man is seized with madness and roams the earth. Cupidity makes a man as restless as a dog.

70. How should fortune dwell in the houses of those who perpetually tell lies? It is like drawing water in a leaky vessel.

71. The house of a virtuous young woman is orderly, she is like as a light shining in a dark room: The house in which a first *wedded* wife dwells is *like as* the place of divine worship.

---

* The rhyme in this line is evidently wrong. Possibly the author wrote.

భిన్న ఘటము నీరు చన్న చందంబున.

Yet many similar blemishes in the present volume must be attributed to the author himself.

ఇంటి యాలు విడిచి యిల జార - కాంతల
వెంట దిరుగు - వాడు వెర్రి వాడు;
పంట చేను విడిచి పరిగె యేరిన యట్లు. వి. ౭౨

రాజ - వరుల కె'ప్పుడు రణ - రంగముల చింత;
పరమ - మునుల కె'ల్ల పరమచింత;
యల్ప - నరుల కె'ల్లన' తివెలపైచింత. వి. ౭౩

తల్లి - దండ్రి మీద దయ లేని పుత్రుండు
పుట్టనే'మి? వాడు గిట్టనే'మి?
పుట్టలోన చెదలు పుట్టదా గిట్టదా? వి. ౭౪

ముందరి పోటులు మాన్పను
మందె'ందై'నాను గలదు' మహి లోపలనే;
నిందల - మాటలు మాన్పెడు
మం దెం' దై'నాను గలదె? మహిలో వేమా ౭౫

---

72. He that leaves his wife at home and roams after incontinent women in the world is a madman. It is like leaving his fruitful field to go and gather mere gleanings.

73. The thoughts of kings are perpetually on the battlefield. Eminent saints are constantly thinking on the Most High. But light men are always thinking on women *alone*.

74. The son who hath no regard for mother and father, what matter though he be born, what though he perish? Do not the white-ants in a hillock come forth and perish *as well as he*?

75. A medicine may always be found somewhere in the world to heal wounds received in front. But hath any remedy been found to heal *the wounds of* slanderous words?

తత్వమె' రుగు - వాడు దైవంబు నె' రుగును ;
సర్వ - సారములను జంపఁ జేయు ;
కదళి మ్రింగు వాడు గరళంబు మ్రింగునా ? వి. ౭౬

నీళ్ల మీఁద బుగ్గ నిలచిన యప్పుడు ;
తళ్లు వేగ వచ్చి తాఁకు గాక ;
విడెపు - కుండకి' ంత విభ్రాంతి పడుదురు ! వి. ౭౭

హేమకార - విద్య నె' రిగిన వారె' ల్ల
వెతలఁ బడని యట్లు విద్య చేత
తత్వమె' రుగు వెనుక తనకు చింతే' లరా ? వి ౭౮

జీవ - భావమె' రుగ జెడదె' న్న టికి మతి ;
దైవమునునె' రుంగ దనరు బుద్ధి ;
తేజము' దయమం' ద దిమిరంబు నిలువదు. వి, ౭౯

---

76. He who knows the truth knows the Divinity, and this will enable him to slay all his lusts. Will he who has swallowed a delicious plantain swallow bitter venom ?

77. When a bubble stands on water, a rapid rush in passing destroys it. Alas ! what affection men feel for the frail earthen vessel *of the body*.

78. Like as all those who comprehend the science of alchymy by reason of that skill suffer no *more* sorrows, so when thou hast learnt the truth thou shalt no more grieve.

79. If thou knowest the nature of life, *and that it consists in the temporary union of soul and body*, never shall thy mind perish *in delusion*. If thou knowest the Deity, wisdom shall shine *within thee* ; after the light hath arisen darkness shall no more remain.

ఆశచేత మనుజులా' యువు ఁగల నాళ్లు
ఁదిరుగుచు' ందురు భ్రమ' ద్రిప్ప లేక ;
ముఱికి భాండమందు ముసరు నీగల భంగి. వి. ౮౦

పర సమి' నుము సోకి బంగారమై' నట్లు ;
కప్పురంబు జ్యోతి గలసిన' ట్లు ;
పుష్పమందు తావి పొసగిన' ట్ల' గు, ముక్తి. వి. ౮౧

కుండ పగిలెనే' ని క్రొత్తది *గొనవచ్చు ;
భూ - తలంబునందు పొందుగాను
కూల బడిన నరుఁడు కుదురుట యరుదయా! వి. ౮౨

జపము బాహ్య - పూజ ఁజాల ఁజేసి పిదప
కపటము విడ లేక కష్ట - నరులు
ముక్తిఁ బొం 'ద లేక మునిఁగిరి తమమున. వి. ౮౩

---

80. Through strong desire do men wander all the days of their life, unable to rid themselves of delusion; like to flies that settle on a vessel defiled *with wine*.

81. As iron by touching the Philosopher's stone becomes gold; like as camphor unites with the lamp, and both become fire; or like as the odor in a flower is united therewith, such is absorption: *it consists in the uniting of our soul with the Divinity*.

82. Though a vessel be broken, a new one is *easily* procured. Is it then marvellous that after a man's death he should acquire *a new body*?

83. After much meditation and external worship wicked men, who cease not from hypocrisy, are unable to attain beatitude, and sink into darkness.

---

* Several manuscripts read గొబ్బున కొనవచ్చు.

ఊర్ధ్వ - లోకమందును' చిత క్రమంబున ;
రూపమే' మి లేక రూఢితోన ;
పరమ - యోగి చూచు, పరమాత్ముడి' తడ' ని. వి. ౮౪

సత్యము' మరి యుండ, జ్ఞానము' మరి యుండు,
జ్ఞానము' మరి యుండ సత్యము ండు
జ్ఞాన సత్యములును సమ మైన ద్విజుండ' గు. వి ౮౫

దానమొ' సంగు కన్న, దేనంబు * మరి హెచ్చు ;
దేనమొ' సంగు కన్న, తెలివి హెచ్చు ;
తెలివి కన్న నాసం † దెగ వేసిన ది హెచ్చు. వి. ౮౬

దొంగ మాటలా' డ, దొరుకునా మోక్షంబు ?
చేత గాని కూతచెల్లదె' పుడు ?
గురువు పద్దు గాదు, గుణహీన మటి ‡ గాక. వి. ౮౭

---

84. In the world above, *after finishing* his holy course, the perfected saint shall in reality behold the Great Spirit, devoid of all form, and say, This is He!

85. If thou be endued with truth, thou shalt attain wisdom; by gaining wisdom, thou shalt attain the truth. He is the regenerate who possesseth wisdom and truth in an equal degree.

86. Meditation is of superior merit to the bestowing of gifts, as understanding is superior to meditation; and to cut off our lusts is superior even to understanding.

87. If thou use the words of hypocrisy, how shalt thou attain beatitude? thy vain babbling shall never pass as good: this is no dignified undertaking, but only a fruitless inclination.

---

* దేనము for ధ్యానము ; a Tadbhava form. † ఆస for ఆశ.

‡ మది for మతి.

గాలి లేని దీప_కళిక చందంబున,
లలు సనుల్లు లేని జలధి రీతి ;
నిశ్చలాత్మ యెన్న నిర్వికారంబున
నుండెనే' ని, ముక్తియండ్రు వేమ. ౮౮
మంట లోహములను, మాను చీలలయందు
ఁబటము గోడల' ందు, ఁబరగ సిసుకఁ
బెట్టిన' ఁటున' ట్లు, ఁబెనఁగు దేహము జీవి. వి. ౮౯
కలుషమె' ల్ల (ఁదెలియు), ఁదల వంపులకు మూల
మ', రయ తత్వమె' ల్లనా' త్మ ఁబుట్టు ;
తెలివిన' ందుకు మరి ధీరుండు గావలె! వి. ౯౦
అనగ ననఁగ రాగమ తిశయిల్లుచు నుండు
తినగ తినగ వేము తీఁపిను' ండు
సాధకమున బనులు సమకూరు ధరలోన. వి. ౯౧

---

88. Like to the flame of a lamp *that is placed* out of the wind—like to the ocean free from defiling whirlpools—is the unagitated soul when free from change. This is named beatitude.§

89. As metals unite with flame, and a spike with wood, and figures with the walls *on which they are painted*, so are the body and living soul united.

90. Know that sin is always the cause of drooping the head ; that all true good originates in the spirit, but to comprehend this requires much firmness.

91. By talking and conversing affection increases : as you continue to eat *even the bitter* Nimba *leaf*, it becomes sweet ; so by practice may we succeed in any art *whatever*.

---

§ Release, freedom, perfection, or salvation ; absorption in the Deity.

స్థూలము కను గుడ్డు' సూక్ష్మంబు కన్పాప'
కంటిపాపను'ండు కారణంబు.
కారణమున బ్రహ్మ - కళ నెరుంగ వలెను. వి. ౯౨

తేనె తెరల జాడ తేనె టీగ యెరుంగు
సుమ - రసంబు జాడ భ్రమర మె'రుఁగు;
పరమ - యోగి జాడ' భక్తుఁడె' రుంగును. వి. ౯౩

అడవి ఁదిరుఁగ లేదు' యాకసమున లేదు,
అవని ఁదీర్థ - యాత్రల'ందు లేదు;
ఒడలు శుద్ధి ఁజేసి' యొడయుని జూడరా! వి. ౯౪

కప్పురంపు మనసు ఁగాంక్షించు యోగికి
జ్ఞాన - దీప - శిఖయుఁ దా నటించు;
కాన వచ్చునా'త్మ - క్రమమాణమై'నిచ్చ. వి. ౯౫

---

92. Large is the eye-ball, minute is the pupil; *yet* in the pupil *alone exists* the source *of vision*: such are the mediums through which we view the Deity.

93. As the bee knows the direction of the hive; and as the humble bee seeks where the sweetest sap is found: so does a devoted spirit seek after the perfected saint.

94. Though *we* roam the wilds, *sanctity* is not in them; nor is it in the sky; nor on earth in the confluence of holy streams. Make thy body pure and thou shalt behold the king.

95. The devout man who longs for a heart *pure as* camphor, shall himself shine as the flame of the lamp of wisdom. By the gradual progress of his soul shall he attain his desire.

3

నీవా' డిన నేనా' డుదు;
నీవు' ండిన నేను నుం' దు, నిర్విణ్ణుడనై;
నీవు దలంచిన ఁదలపుదు
నీవు నగిన నేను నగుదు! నిజముగ వేమా. ౯౬

నీరు కారమా' యె, కారంబు నీరా' యె;
కారమైన నీరు కారమా' యె
కారమందు నీరు కడు రమ్యమై' యుండు. వి. ౯౭

శివుని యనుభవంబు సృష్టిలోపల లేక,
సంశయంబు చెడదు సాధకులకు;
చెలగు దివ్వె లేక చీకటి వాయునా? వి. ౯౮

ఇంద్రియముల చేతనె' గ్గొందుచు' ఁడెడు
వెర్రి* మనుజుడే' ల వెదకు శివుని?
ఇంద్రియముల రోసి యీశుని జూడుడీ. వి. ౯౯

96. What thou sayest, *O God*, I will say! where thou dwellest I will remain enwrapt: my thoughts shall be like to thine; and when thou smilest I will also smile.

97. Water becomes saltpetre, and saltpetre turns into water; nitrous water is converted into nitre: so strong is the attraction between a salt and a fluid.

98. If, while on earth, he attain not the enjoyment of God, never shall the aspirant be freed from doubt. Can a house be luminous devoid of a candle?

99. Why should the fool, who is still agitated by his lusts, seek after God? Forsake your passions, and ye shall see him.

---

* In the present volume I have excluded the letter ఱ for reasons given in "Telgugu Prosody Explained." Thus వెఱ్ఱి is printed వెర్రి. We may be sure that Vemana never used the letter ఱ

కడుపు నిండ సుధను గ్రమముతోఁ ద్రావిన
పాల మీఁద నేల పాఱు మనసు?
తత్వమెఱుఁగ వెనుక తత్వంబు లేటికో? వి. ౧౦౦

ఉత్తమో - త్తముండు తత్వజ్ఞుఁడే (ల మీఁద)
మహిమఁ జూపు వాఁడు మధ్యముండు.
వేషధారి, యుదర - పోషకుఁడధముండు. వి. ౧౦౧

హృదయమందు నున్న యీశుని దెలియక,
శిలల కెల్ల మ్రొక్కు జీవులార !
శిలలనేమి యుండు, జీవులందే కాక ? వి. ౧౦౨

గంగి - గోవు పాలు గంటెడైనను జాలు ;
కడవెడైన నేమి ఖరము పాలు ;
భక్తిఁ గలుగు కూడు పట్టెడైనను జాలు. వి. ౧౦౩

---

100. If one have drunk his belly full of nectar, how should his mind run upon milk? When we know the *divine* essence, to what end are other beings?*

101. The best of the excellent on earth is he who knoweth the truth; he who displays his own greatness is in the middle state; and he who wears a *religious* garb to nourish his belly is the lowest of all.

102. O! ye who, ignorant of the God who dwells in the heart, bow down to all stones, ye mere animals! what is there in a stone *superior to* what is in a living body!

103. A single spoonful of milk from a good cow is enough; of what use is a pailful of ass's millk? a single handful of food given with faith (zeal or affection) is enough.

---

* See note on verse III.

బండ మీఁద చెలమ పాటించి త్రవ్విన,
నలయికె' క్కుడౌ' ను, ఆశ లేదు;
గుంట పట్టు చెలమ కులము' ద్ధరించు రా. వి. ౧౦౪

కాకి - గూటి లోన కోకిలమన్న' ట్లు
భ్రమరము' గుచు పురువు బ్రతికిన' ట్లు;
గురుని ఁగొల్చు వెనక, గురువు తానౌ' నయా. వి.

మాట దిద్ద వచ్చు' మరి యొగ్గు లేకుండ,
దిద్ద వచ్చు రాయి, తిన్నగాను;
మనసు దిద్ద రాదు, మహానె' ంత వారికి. వి. ౧౦౬

మనసునందు ముక్తి మలయుచును' ండంగ,
మనసునె' రుగ లేక, మనుజులె' ల్ల,
మనసున' ంట లేక, మాయమై పోదురు. వి. ౧౦౭

---

104. If you painfully dig a well in a rock *devoid of a spring*, you will suffer great weariness, but not gain your desire : but a pit dug in low ground will support a tribe.

105. Like a cuckoo lives in a crow's nest ; like the worms live that are hidden by a wasp ; * is he who honors a teacher : he shall himself become a master.

106. Speech may be corrected *so as to be* without irregularity ; a stone may be carved into a fine form ; but the mind can never be altered, no, not in the best of men.

107. *Though the principles in wich* beatitude *originates* exist in *our own* heart, all men who are unable to know their hearts, and to restrain their minds, vanish *in death*.

* It is imagined in India that the caterpillers placed by a wasp in its nest themselves turn into wasps.

మనసు ముక్తి యనుచు, మదినెఱుంగఁగ లేరు,
మనసుచేత దగిలి మాయఁబైరి;
మనసు తానైన మర్మజ్ఞుఁడగు యోగి. వి. ౧౦౮
మదినెఱిగిన వాని మహిఁ గానమెందును,
మదినెఱుంగు నరుడు మహిని నరుదు;
వెదకి తనువులోన వేడ్కతో నినుఁ జూచు. వి. ౧౦౯
బ్రహ్మమును యెరుగదు భావమందుండెనా,
తనువు గుడిగఁ జేసి, తన్ను నిలిపి,
లోకబుద్ధి విడిచి, లోఁజూపుఁ జూడరా. వి.
నిన్నుఁ జూచుచుండ నిండును తత్వంబు;
తన్నుఁ జూచుచుండ తగులు మాయ
నిన్ను నెఱిగినపుడె తన్నుఁ దానెఱుంగును. వి.

108. They cannot learn that the heart is *the source of* perefction; they are entangled in their lusts and perish; he who is converted into pure mind is the saint who knows the *great* secret.

109. Nowhere do we see one who knows his own heart; he who knows his heart is rarely found. If he search, he shall with joy find Thee, *O god,* even in the body.

110. The mind cannot see God as long as it is in this life: but convert thy body into a temple, and restrain thyself: give up all worldly thoughts, and see him with thy internal eye.

111. By looking to Thee is wisdom * perfected; by looking to ourselves we fall into delusion; when we know Thee we shall know ourselves.

---

*The word *tatwam* is extremely indefinite, and is translated in various modes, as the import of the passage requires; it may be often rendered "That which is" (the highest of blessings or wisdom); the obscure "To ev" of Socrates; "The truth," or true good in general. Elsewhere it is equivalent to Nature or to Essence. See verse 100.

గాలి గాలిఁ గలసె, గగనంబు గగనంబు,
మన్ను మన్నుఁ గలసె, మంట మంట;
నీరు నీటఁ గలసె, నిర్మలంబై యుండె. వి. ౧౧౨

వెదుక వెదుక దొరుకు వేదాంత వేద్యుండు;
వెదుకు వానిఁ దాను వెదుకుచుండు;
వెదుక నేర్చినట్టి వెరవర్లు గలరకో? వి. ౧౧౩

తను వలచినఁ దా వలచును
తను వలవక యున్నఁ దన్నుఁ దా వలవడి [లక్ష.]
తనదు పటాటోపంబులు
తన మాయలు పనికి రావు [ధరలో వేమా]! ౧౧౪

---

112. *In the dissolution, at death, of the five corporeal elements* air returns to air, ether to ether, earth to earth, flame to flame, and water to water; *thus does the spirit* attain purity.

113. By searching and seeking, he who knoweth the scripture * is found: he seeketh the man who seeketh him; alas! are there any who are wise and seek him?

114. If we love him, he will love us; if we love not him, never will he love us: all our display, all our hypocrisy, will be of no avail [in the world].

* God, the Supreme Teacher.

స్వానుభూతి లేక, శాస్త్ర - వాసనల చే,
సంశయంబు చెడదు సాధకునకు ;
చిత్ర - దీపమునను ఁజీకటి చెడనట్లు. వి. ౧౧౫

శాంతమున సకల కార్యము
సంతోషంబునను బొందు ; సత్యము జయమౌ ;
పంతము చెల్లును ; ధర్మజు -
డెంతేసి ప్రయాసముల జయించెను, వేమా! ౧౧౬

ఉర్వి - జనులు, పరమ - యోగీశ్వరుని ఁజూచి,
తెగడు వారు గాని, తెలియ లేరు
అమృతమాది రుచుల హస్తమే మెరుగును ? వి.

---

115. Without personal experience, the mere savor of the scripture will not remove the fears of the aspirant ; * as darkness is never dispelled by a *mere* painted flame.

116. By gentleness is every object pleasantly obtained: truth shall become victorious : our vow shall be accomplished. How great were the difficulties overcome by *the gentle* Dharma-Raz ! †

117. When the sons of earth see the holy saint ‡ they revile him, but cannot understand him. Can the hand discern ambrosia from other tastes ?

---

* The three terms Sadhaca, Sadhana, and Sadhyam in Indian philosophy signify the agent, the instrument, and the object of any act ; as mind-deliberation, and execution; or the thinker, his hand, and the work produced. The relative senses of the three words (with their numerous derivatives) may be recollected by the following hexameter :

Sadhaca, Sadhana, Sadhyam, Ego, calamusque, liberque. Or we might read,

Sadhaca, Sadhana, Sadhyam, Scriptor, penna, libellus.

† An allusion to a tale in the Maha Bharata.

‡ Lit. The Lord of consummate devotion.

పురుషుడె' న్నిగతులఁ బుట్టింది, * మొదలుగ,
పాప చింతఁ జేయు పామరమున
మదిని గుంటి కుక్క మాంసముఁ దిన్నట్లు. వి. ౧౧౮

అంకిలె' రిగి మాటలా' డ నేర్చిన' పుడె,
పిన్న పెద్ద తనములె, న్ననేల' ల?
పిన్న చేతి దివ్వె పెద్దగా వెలుగదా? వి. ౧౧౯

మొదటఁ బోయు నీరు [మొగి] బీజములకె' క్కు,
మొదటికు' రుక వేగ మొలక లె' త్తు;
మొలక పృథివి బెరిగి వెలయును వృక్షంబు. వి. ౧౨౦

---

118. However often he be re-born in the human form, stupidly does he meditate on sin alone: like a lame dog who in imagination eats flesh.

119. When one has learnt to speak prudently, why should we think of his youth or age? May not a lamp burn bright though held in the hand of an infant?

120. The water at first poured on the seed affects it, reaching the root; soon it raises a sprout; the shoot grows in the soil, and the tree comes to light.

---

* For పుట్టింది, a form of the verbal noun which belongs to the గ్రామ్యం or colloquial dialect, we might substitute (పుట్టుక) as a more poetical గ్రాంథిక from; it would not, however, be expedient to alter the text wherever the metre, the grammar, or the style may have been left imperfect by the author. Verse 122 contains two errors in elision; which, indeed, might be remedied by reading సారమొ'క్కటియగు, and భావ్యుడొ'క్కండగు; bur critical exactitude is not to be expected in an author who disregarded elegance of style.

మగని కాలమందు మగువ కష్టించిన,
సుతుల కాలమందు సుఖముఁ బొందు.
కలిమి లేమి రెండు గలవెంత వారికి.
బలిమి, పుత్ర బలిమి బలిమి, వేమ. ౧౨౧

ఆరు రుచులు వేరు సారంబు ఒక్కటి ;
సత్య - నిష్ఠ వేరు సత్యమొకటి ;
పరమ ఋషులువేరు, భావ్యుండు ఒక్కడు. వి. ౧౨౨

తారకంబుఁ జూచు దారి వేరే కల్దు ;
సమము గాను జూడ, ఁజక్కఁబడును ;
వెర్ర గాను జూడ, వెలుగెల్ల బారురా! వి. ౧౨౩

సజ్జనముల చెలిమి ఁజాలింపఁగా రాదు ;
ప్రకృతినెరుగకున్న, భక్తి లేదు.
పలువలెట్టి రీతి భక్తి నిల్పుదురయా? వి. ౧౨౪

121. If in the time of her husband's life a woman labours, she shall enjoy comfort in the time of her sons; all, however great, participate in wealth and poverty. The strength of strong sons is the greatest of all.

122. The six flavors * are diverse, but taste is one; various are the creeds regarding truth, but truth is one: and saints differ among themselves, while he on whom they meditate is one.

123. If thou look *to God* through the *appointed* means, there is a certain method *of attaining to him:* if thou look steadily to him, it shall become straight; but if thou look to him as a fool, all his light shall depart.

124. Cease not from friendship with the good: till we understand our *fallen* nature, we have no faith; how shall a sinner attain firmness in faith?

* *Viz.* salt, acid, sour, sweet, bitter, astringent; *uppu, pulusu, caram,* [illegible]*ttpi, chedu, ogaru.*

ఇట్టి కనుల బ్రహ్మమె ట్లు చూడఁగ వచ్చు?
చూచు కనులు వేరు, చూపు వేరు.
చూపు లోన నుంచి చూడంగ వలవదా? వి. ౧౨౫

దూలములను బోలు దురవస్థలను ఎల్ల
రోసి, యాసల న్ని గోసివేసి
వాసనను తెలిసిన వాడెపో, బ్రహ్మంబు! వి. ౧౨౬

మన్నును దినుమంటె, మండేరు జనులార?
మంటి లోని మేలు మరువనేల?
నీళ్ల లోని మేలు, నిఖిలమై యుండురా! వి. ౧౨౭

---

125. With such eyes as these how can we view the Deity? the eyes that see him are different, the vision is diverse. Must not we look to him with an internal eye?

126. He who hates all these evil periods of life that are *burthensome* as a beam; and who cuts off all his passions; who knows *the true value of* his feelings, he (go to) is *become endued with* the divine spirit.*

127. If it is said "Eat earth"† ye flame with rage; why do ye forget the good ye derive from the soil? The benefits of water pervade the world *without acknowledgment.*

---

* The versification, in this author (as here exemplified) is sometimes prosaic: the thought obscure; and the mode of argument inconclusive some of these defects evidently originate in the ignorance of transcribers: with others, the author must himself be charged. The elision (sandhi) in the first line (see note on verse 118) being omitted దురవస్థలెల్లను might be adopted as a more grammatical form.

† A common curse; a pun is here intended. మండేరు is *gramyam* for మండుదురు. See note on verse 118.

జీవమే డనుండు? భావమెక్కడనుండు?
కాపురంబు యేడఁ గదిసి యుండు?
తనరుచున్న రెంటి స్థలమేల తెలియరు? వి. ౧౨౮

ధనము గూడఁ బెట్టి, ధర్మంబు సేయక,
తాను దినక లెస్స దాచుగాక,
తేనెనీఁగ గూర్చి తెరవరికీయ్యదా? వి. ౧౨౯

ఇచ్చే వారల సంపద
హెచ్చేదే కాని, లేమి యేలా కలుగున్?
అచ్చెలమ నీళ్లు చల్లిన,
విచ్చలవిడినూరుచుండు, వినరా వేమా! ౧౩౦

---

128. Where does life reside? where does thought dwell? what place is their habitation? why can ye not perceive the evident * abode of these two *principles*.

129. He heaps up wealth, and gives none in charity: he consumes it not himself, but hides it! Will not the bee that stores up honey yield it *by force* to the traveller?

130. The wealth of liberal men shall always increase; poverty shall never befall them; when that † well has poured forth its waters, again shall they be plentifully produced.

---

* The verb తనరు is here only a పాదపూర్ణక, being inserted merely to fill the metre: it usually signifies *to be manifest, to appear*; and hence *to be, to exist*. ఏడ also is *gramyam* for ఎక్కడ. The elision is here neglected which ought to take place in the second line, *viz.*, కాపురంబె క్కడ.

† The author perhaps wrote అచెలము: but the uniformity requisite in the *prasa* syllable demands this alteration in spelling.

పాలఁ గలయు నీరు పాలై రాజిల్లు,
నదియుఁ బాంబ యోగ్యమైన యట్లు
సాధు సజ్జనముల సాంగత్యముల చేత,
మూఢ జనుడు ముక్తి నొనయు వేమ! ౧౩౧

చెడిన మానవులను చేపట్టి రక్షించి,
కడకు దేర్చినట్టి ఘనుఁడు, తలప,
కడగి పుణ్యమైన కడు శివ - సన్నిధి,
నెడ తెగకయ యుందు రెపుడు వేమ! ౧౩౨

131. Water mingled with milk bears the appearance of milk; and thus becomes acceptable in sacred rites: thus, by intercourse with the pure and excellent shall even the foolish attain perfection.*

132. The rich man who takes the destitute by the hand and rescues him, shall ultimately, in the presence of the glorious Siva, † shall unceasingly dwell in *happiness.*

---

* See note on verse 88.

† The term *Siva* is generally used in this author for God: but in several passages he derides the personages of the Hindu triad: and evidently believed in one God alone. There is a దుస్సంధిమి in the third line; also in verse 134. The reader will perceive such flaws as he proceeds withou their being pointed out.

ఒకరి నోరుఁ గొట్టి, యొకరు భక్షింతురు,
వారు నోరు మిత్తి వరుస గొట్టు ;
చేఁప పిండునే' ల చేఁపలు చంపును ?
జనుడు చేప పిండుఁ జంపు వేమ! ౧౩౩

కనులు పోవు వాడు కాళ్లు పోయిన వాడు
ఉభయుల' రయు, ఁగూడి యుండిన' ట్లు,
పేద పేదఁ గూడి పెనగొని యుండును. వి. ౧౩౪

పరగ రాతి గుండు పగలఁ గొట్టగ వచ్చు,
కొండల' న్ని పిండి గొట్ట వచ్చు,
కఠిన చిత్తు మనసు కరిగింపఁగా రాదు. వి. ౧౩౫

---

133. They will strike a man on the face, * and devour his substance ; they in turn shall be smitten on the mouth by *the goddess* of death : as fishes, preying on the fishy tribe, are destroed by man *in just retribution.*

134. He who has lost his eyes, and he who has lost his legs, unite *to aid one another* ; so the beggar unites with the poor man.

135. A stone ball may he broken, the very hills may be reduced to dust ; but the heart of the cruel man can be melted by nothing !

---

* That is deprive him of his rights ; the word *ocaru* here implies generality ; indefinitely, one or another. మిత్తి is written for మృత్యు This verse appears to be translated from the following, in the Naishadham. (Viyogini metre.)

అబల స్వకులాశి నో ఝషాన్ నిజనీడద్రుమ పీడినః ఖగాన్
అనవద్యతృణాది నో మృగాన్ మృగయాఘాయ న భూభృతాం ఘ్నతాం.

అంత కొరత ఁదీరి యతిశయ కాముఁడై
నిన్ను నమ్మి చాల నిష్ఠ తోడ,
నిన్ను ఁగొల్వ ముక్తి నిశ్చయముగ ఁగల్గు. వి. ౧౩౬

తత్వము తిరమై'న, తావుల వెదకుచు,
తాను తత్వమగును, తత్వ - యోగి
తలపుల'న్ని యుడుగ, తానె, పో, తత్వంబు! వి. ౧౩౭

మాటలా'డ వేరె మనసు కొలది వేరె;
యొడలి గుణము వేరె యోజ వేరె;
యెట్లు గల్గు ముక్తి యేలాగు తనలాగు? వి. ౧౩౮

---

136. He who, free from fault, and full of love, believeth on Thee and with all austerity worshippeth Thee; he shall certainly attain release (mucti: see v. 83, n.)

137. When he is well grounded in the truth (*tatwa*), he searcheth it in *every* place, and, united with holiness, shall be transformed into it; all his *vain* thoughts shall be done away; and he (go to) shall be perfect.*

138. Talking is one thing, and the temper of the mind is another; the qualities of the body *tend* one way, and our intention another! How shall we attain salvation! and what path is this we are pursuing?

---

* The word *tatwam* (see note on verse III) is here used in three senses translated by *truth*, *holiness*, and *perfection*. తిరము *is written for* స్థిరము.

వెలది చక్కఁదనము వెరవైన యీడును
విభుని కరుణ లేక వితగనుండు ;
నీదు కరుణ లేక నేర్పులు కొఱగావు! వి. ౧౩౯
ఎంత కష్టముండున' ంత పాపపు చింత ;
చింత చేత మిగులఁ జివుకు మనసు ;
చింత లేక యున్న చెడని సంపద జూచు. వి. ౧౪౦
ఎన్నాళ్లును దానుండును
యెన్నాళ్లును దాను నేర్చి యెన్నిట వెలయుఁ ;
కొన్నాళ్లకుఁ దాఁ జన్నను *
మన్నా 'యెను విద్య లెల్ల! [మహిలో] వేమా. ౧౪౧
ధనమొచ్చిన్న మనమొచ్చును,
మనమొచ్చిన దుర్గుణంబు మానక యొచ్చుఁ ;
ధనముడిగిన మనసుడుగును ;
మనముడిగిన దుర్గుణంబు మానును వేమా! ౧౪౨

139. As the beauty of a woman and her lovely bloom, if devoid of grace in her husband's eyes, are all unprofitable ; so, devoid of Thy grace, all our skill is fruitless !

140. In proportion to a man's difficulties are his wicked devices ; by *such* thoughts the mind is much weakened ; if devoid of anxiety, he possesses an imperishable treasure.

141. However many days he lives, however long he is learning, and however he is distinguished, in a few days he dies, and is turned to earth, with all his skill.

142. As wealth increases, inclinations increase ; with our inclinations our evil nature fails not to be aggravated : when wealth ceases, our lusts leave us : and with those lusts are our bad dispositions diminished.

* జన్నను for చనును to preserve the metre.

విన వలెనె' వ్వరు చెప్పిన ;
వినిన' ంతనె తిమక - పడక వివరింప వలెఁ :
విని కని వివరము ‹దెలిసిన
మనుజుడు పో నీతి - పరుడు, మహిలో వేమా. ౧౪౩

ఈ కపట నాటకంబును,
ఈ కపటపు చదువుల' న్ని యింపు దలిర్పఁ
ఏ కపటా' త్ముడు సేసెనొ,
యా కపటా' త్మునకు మ్రొక్కి, యలరుము వేమా.

ఎండ వేళ చీకటి' కమై యున్నట్లు,
నిండు కుండ నీరు నిలిచిన' ట్లు,
దండిని ‹బరమా' త్మ తత్వంబు దెలియరో! వి. ౧౪౫

---

143. Whoever speaks, hear him; while listening be not wroth, but examine it well with discrimination:* if, by listening and viewing, he discovers the truth, (go to) a man shall become excellent in wisdom.

144. Him, the hidden spirit, who created this well-contrived mystic dance, and delights in these recondite studies, † worship that inscrutable spirit, and rejoice in him. O Vema!

145. Like as when the sun shines *clearly*, and darkness hides itself; ‡ and as when *clear* water fills a vase; so *fully and clearly* let us comprehend the essence of the supreme spirit.

---

* The sense would appear to require [illegible] if the metre admitted instead of *vivarimpa*: but the verse appears in only one of my manuscripts. The last line was written thus: మనుజుడెయానీతి, &c., which gives no clear meaning.

† Perhaps we should read చేష్టలన్ని for చదువులన్ని.

‡ See the Vasu Charitra: book 4. verse 6.

ఎండిన మూనొ' కట' డవిని
ఉండినన' ంద'గ్ని పుట్టి యూడ్చును చెట్లఁ ;
దండి గల వంశ మెల్లను
చండాలుండొ' కడు పుట్టి చదుపును వేమా ! ౧౪౬

శిష్య - వర్గమునకు శివుఁ జూప నేరక
కాని మతము లోనఁ గలుపు నట్టి
గురుని యెరుకన', రయు, గుడ్డె' ద్దు జొన్న, రా. వి.

ఇంటి లోని ధనము, "యిది నాది" యనుచును,
మంటి లోన దాచు, మంకు జీవి !
కొంటఁ బోడు వెంట గుల్ల కాసును రాదు. వి. ౧౪౮

---

146. If there be one dry tree in a forest, it will produce flame *by friction* and sweep away all the rest : thus if a base wretch * be born in a noble race, he will destroy it all.

147. The teacher † who is unable to show the path of holiness to his disciples, and plunges them in an evil creed, his wisdom is like that of a bullock entangled in a field of maize.‡

148. The wicked wretch § considers the wealth in his house as his own for ever, and hides it in the earth; yet he cannot carry a *cauri* or a farthing with him when he dies.

---

* Lit. a *Chandala*, which answers to "*heathen*," and is generally applied to outcasts.

† Guru, a teacher, doctor, or precepter in religion.

‡ Also called cholum the stalk of which is sometimes ten feet high.

§ జీవి literally, an *animal* or *brute*; a common expression of Vemana in such pages.

దేశ వేషములను తేట సేయక దేవు
డా'త్మ లోనను ండున' నగి పెనగి ;
వేసము' రసి చూడ, గ్రాసంబు కొఱకయో ! వి. ౧౪౯

మిరప గింజఁ జూడ మీఁద నల్లగను, ండు ;
కొఱికి చూడ, లోన చురుకుము' నును ;
సజ్జనులగు వారి సారమి, ట్టులను' ండు. వి. ౧౫౦

పర్వత - వన - వాసి, పరిణామ వర్తన,
కూప - వాసికె' ట్లు గుఱుతు పడును ?
బ్రహ్మ - నిష్ఠు వెంట ప్రాకృతుడ' రుగునా ? వి. ౧౫౧

---

149. God regards not * our country or our garb; he dwells in the soul, intimately entwined therewith; *an assumed* garb † is merely worn for the sake of the belly.

150. If you look at a grain of pepper, it is externally black; if you bite it, you perceive ‡ that internally it is pungent. Thus *imperceptible* is the worth of the excellent.

151. How can the conduct—so different from his own §—of the hermit who abides in the mountains and wilds be comprehended by him who dwells in the pit of secularity? will the natural man follow after him whose practice is godlike?

---

* తేటసేయక would appear erroneous! but the correct reading is not easily conjectured.

† As that worn by hermits and religious beggars. In this line వేస is written for వేష to preserve the prasa-yati rhyme.

‡ To see: cucu is applied to the perception of all the senses.

§ Lit. of diverse conduct.

కస్తురి యట చూడ, కాంతి నల్లగను' ండు ;
పరిమళించు దాని పరిమళంబు ;
గురువు లైన వారి గుణములీ' లాగు, రా. వి. ౧౫౨

దొంగతనము రంకు దొరసి యుండు జగతి ;
రంకులాడికి' ంత శంక ?బుట్టు ;
దొంగకె('న్న) రే - వెలుంగొ' ప్ప కాన' ట్టు. వి

గురువు లేక విద్య గురుతుగా దొరకదు,
నృపతి లేక భూమి తృప్తిగాదు ;
గురువు విద్య లేక గురుతర - ద్విజుడొ' నె ?వి. ౧౫౪

---

152. Look closely at musk; its hue *indeed* is dark, but its fragrance perfumes *all things*. Thus *hidden* are the virtues of men of weight.

153. Theft and whoredom are alike in the world; the adultress is full of apprehension like the thief, who dares not view the beauty of moonlight.

154. Without a teacher learning cannot be accurately gained; as without a ruler the earth is not nourished: without teacher and learning how can one become distinguished among the twice-born?*

---

* *Dwija*; generally translated, *a Bramin*; because supposed to be *regenerated* by the rite of wearing the scared thread. Vema uses this word in a more extensive sense.

అల్ప - సుఖములె’ ల్లనా’ శించి మనుజుండు,
బహుళ దుఃఖములను బాధపడును ;
పర - సుఖంబు నొంది, బ్రతుకంగ నేరడు. వి. ౧౫౫

కాల - వశము ఁబట్టి, కర్మ - జీవుల పిండు *
మత్తుల’ గుచును మద - మత్తులై’ రి;
మత్తులైన జనుల మనసే’ టి మనఃసయా? వి. ౧౫౬

[కడగి †] వట్టి యాస కడతేర నివ్వదు
ఇడుములందు ఁజొట్టి యీడ్చు గాని;
పుడమి జనుల భక్తి బొడమంగ నియ్యదు. వి. ౧౫౭

పాల లోన పులుసు లీలతోఁ గలసిన,
విరిసి తునకల’ గును, విరివిగాను ;
తెలివి మనము లోన దివ్య తత్వము ‡ తేట. వి ౧౫౮

---

155. The man who longs after trifling comforts suffers the grief of many sorrows; it is out of his power to attain the highest of bliss, and live *for ever*.

156. Sinful creatures are all subject to time; they are intoxicated by the lusts they delight in; ah! what kind of heart is the heart of a drunken man?

157. Vain desire suffers not to attain our end; it only plunges us in troubles, and drags us along; it prevents faith from being born in men.

158. If you mingle an acid with milk, it will separate, cracking into pieces; thus does the divine influence ‡ divide the understanding heart.

---

* For జీవులురొల్ల as it stands in the M.S.

† కడగి merely fills the verses.

‡ *Tatwam.* See on verses 111 and 137.

దేహము లెస్సగను'ండిన,
పోహణ - తత్వంబుల'న్ని పొందుగ దెలుసుఁ;
దేహము బడలిక బడినను,
పోహణ - తత్వములు [వచ్చి] పొందవు, వేమా. ౧౫౯

అధికుడై'న రాజు * యల్పుని ఁజేపట్ట,
వాని మాట చెల్లు వసుధలోన
గణకులో'ప్పియు'న్న గవ్వలు చెల్లవా? వి. ౧౬౦

ధర్మమ'† రసి పూని ధర్మ రాజా'దులు,
నిర్మలంపు ప్రౌఢి ‡ నిల్పు కొనిరి;
ధర్మమే నృపులకు తారక §- యోగంబు. వి. ౧౬౧

---

159. If the body be well, the real nature of our course is clearly seen; but when the body falls into weakness, we cannot perceive the truth of our state.

160. If a mighty prince takes a light man by the hand, his word will pass *current* in the world; if merchants own them, are not even shells accepted *for money*?

161. By practising what was right, † did Dharma Raz and other warriors maintain their spotless heroism.‡ Righteousness is to all rulers the means of *attaining* salvation.§

---

* Error in Sandhi: see on 132.

† *Dharmam*: that which is peculiarly *right*, due, or befitting; as an imperative duty: righteousness; duty; id quod *fas*. It is thus distinguished from punyam, which implies *merit* acquired by the action.

‡ *Praudhi*: maturity, well-grounded confidence, or just pretensions.

§ More literally "the ground or basis of attainment:" mystic writers, of whom Vemana is one, use this word (taraca) for the "attainment or enjoyment of the deity after absorption."

దానములను సేయ ధర చేతులా'డక,
బహు ధనంబుఁ గూర్చి పాఁతి పెట్టి,
తుదను దండుగని'డి మొదలు చెడు నరుడు. వి. ౧౬౨

నిత్యంబు కాని యొడలికి,
నిత్యము దుఃఖంబుఁ బడును, [నిరతము ధరలో;] *
నిత్యా'నందపు పదవికి
నిత్యంబును దుఃఖ పడగ నేరరు, వేమా! ౧౬౩

విను; వివేకమ నెడు వింత గొడ్డలి చేత,
న'లయు విద్య యనెడు నడవి నరికి,
తెలివి యనెడు గొప్ప దీపంబు చేపట్టి,
ముక్తిఁ జూడ వచ్చు, మొనసి వేమ. ౧౬౪

---

162. He will not move his hands to bestow gifts; he collects much wealth, and buries it; ultimately he shall pay penalty; the man shall be ruined root *and branch.*

163. For this body, devoid of perpetuity, they bear perpetual pain; but never will they take any pains to attain the abode of eternal bliss.

164. Hear! if with the admirable axe discrimination, thou cut down the forest of ignorance, holding in thy hand the great lamp *that is* called understanding, then shalt thou see † perfection.

---

* The words bracketed merely fill up the measure.

† Or, attain. On mucti. v. n. v. 88.

ఎక్కడి సుతులె'? క్కడి సతు.
లె?'క్కడి బంధువులు, సఖులు? నెక్కడి భృత్యుల్?
డొక్కు బడి పోవు వేళల,
చక్కటికిసి నెవరు రారు, సహజము వేమా. ౧౬౫

పాల నీరు క్రమము పరగ హంస యెరుంగు ;
నీరు పాల క్రమము నెమలికే' ల ? *
అజ్ఞుడైన వాడున' ల శివునె' రుగునా? వి. ౧౬౬

కన్నులందు మదము గప్పి కానరు గాని,
నిరుడు ముందటే' డు, నిన్న మొన్న,
దగ్ధులైన వారు తమకంటె తక్కువా? వి. ౧౬౭

---

165. Where are sons or wives; where are relations; where are friends or servants † at the time when we perish? none of them will approach us: this is their nature.

166. The swan alone can distinguish water when mingled with milk: ‡ how should the peacock distinguish *these fluids*? and how shall the ignorant man discern the deity from his own works?

167. They cover their eyes with fatness, and cannot see: but are those who were burnt *on the funeral pyre* (last year, or the year before; yesterday, or the day before) inferior to these, *so blind in their pride*?

---

* False elision: see on verse 132.

† *i. e.*, What have they to do with us.

‡ This is the common idea regarding the *hamsa*: often translated *famingo* and *goose*; but it is acknowledged to be a creature no longer to be found; and may be best translated the *phœnix*, being a fabulous bird to which all that is superlatively excellent or beautiful is compared.

దీపంబు లేని యింటను
రూపంబుల(దెలియ లేరు, రూఢిగ తమలో ;
దీపమ'గు తెలివి గలిగియు,
పాపంబుల మరుగు త్రోవ(బడుదురు, వేమా. ౧౬౮

ఏరు దాటి మెట్ట కే'గిన పురుషుండు,
పుట్టి సరకు(గొనక పోయిన'ట్లు
యోగ-పురుషుడే'ల యొడలు(బొటించురా ? వి.

మంటి కుండ వంటి మాయ శరీరంబు
చచ్చునె ; న్నడైన(జావ'దాత్మ ;
ఘటము లె'న్నియైన గగనంబె యేకమే. వి. ౧౭౦

మాయ'ను చెర - సాల, మనస'ను గొలుసాను ;
భేదమ'నెడు బొండ బెరసి యుండు ;
యిట్టి బద్ధ - జీవి కె'న్నడు మోక్షంబు ? వి. ౧౭౧

168. In a house without a lamp they cannot clearly perceive each others countenances; if you possess the light of understanding, why do you fall into the dark path of sin?

169. The man who has crossed a river and reached the shore cares no longer for the *hide-sewn* boat; why should the man who has attained *happiness* trouble himself about the body?

170. This false body, like an earthen vessel, will die: never shall the soul die; however many vessels there be, *there is but* one expanse *into which they are ultimately resolved.*

171. We are imprisoned in delusion; our inclinations are as chains; *empty* distinctions are the shackles attached to us: when shall be the deliverance from this life of bondage?

---

* The creed in which Vama believed teaches that all things are in common as beings, whether human or divine (to use the words of Pope).

"All are but parts of one stupendous whole,
Whose body nature is, and God the soul."

ఎరుక కన్నను సుఖమే' లోకమున లేదు,
యెరుక నెరుగ నెవ' నికె' రుక లేదు ;
యెరుక సాటి యెరుక యెరుకయే తత్వంబు, వి. ౧౭౨

కని యుండి కాన లేర ట
విని యుండియు వినగ లేరు విస్మయమే మో
"కని గుడ్డియు విని చెవుడం"
చ' నున' ది నిజ' మయ్యె జగమున' ఁదున, వేమా. ౧౭౩

ఊరకు' ంట ఁదెలియను' త్తమ యోగంబు,
మానసంబు కలిమి మధ్యమంబు ;
నాసనా' ది విధులున' ధమ యోగంబు, రా. వి. ౧౭౪

మనసు ఁబూని గెల్చి మనసులో సుఖయించి
కడకు మోక్ష పదము ఁగనును వాడు ;
చెట్టు ఁబెట్ట ఫలము చేకూరకు' ండునా ? వి. ౧౭౫

172. In no world is there a blessing greater than wisdom : none possesses wisdom but he who recognizes *its value*. Knowledge is comparable to itself alone, Wisdom is (tatwa) the chief good.

173. Seeing they cannot see; hearing they cannot hear ! what pride is this ? *the saying* is verified, that "blind is his sight, and deaf is his hearing."

174. Quietism is the highest means of attaining *absorption :* the possession of intellect is the middle grade: postures and other *superstitious rites* are the lowest degree of worship.

175. He who undertakes to subdue his heart shall find comfort therein: at last he shall see the abode of beautitude (mocsha) shall not he who plants a tree obtain its fruit ?

మాట లాడ వచ్చు మనసు నిల్వగ రాదు;
తెలుప వచ్చుఁ దన్నుఁ దెలియ రాదు;
సురియఁ బట్ట వచ్చు శూరుఁడు గా రాదు. వి. ౧౭౬

చూపు నెలయఁ జేసి, సూక్ష్మంపు వత్తిచే
చిత్తమ' నెడు దివ్వె, చెన్ను పరచి,
పాపమ' నెడు తిమిర మే' పారఁ బాపని
పాప జాతి గురుఁడు, పశువు వేమ. ౧౭౭

గురువు చిల్ల - గింజ; 'కుంభమీ' దేహంబు;
ఆత్మ - కలుష - పంకమ' డుగుఁ బట్ట,
తెలిసి విరిచెనే' ని దివ్యా - మృతము తేరు. వి. ౧౭౮

---

176. It is easy to talk, but hard to the mind; we may teach others, but cannot ourselves understand: it is easy to lay hold on the sword, but hard to become valiant.

177. The teacher, *of sinful nature, who cannot clear thine eyes, and with the subtle flame † illumine the lamp of thy heart: who cannot dissipate the darkness of sin, *this teacher* is *no better than* a brute.

178. The teacher is the clearing nut; ‡ the vessel is this body; if the impurities of thy soul sink like mud; through this separation, caused by wisdom, shall divine nectar § be produced.

---

* Guru or Master, v. 147. n. † Lit. The wick.

‡ The nut called *strychnos potatorum*—in Sanskrit *calaca*—which has the property, here alluded to, of cleansing water, if rubbed in the vessel.

§ *Amrit*: signifying nectar as well as water.

గురుడ నగా మొదలంతరు ;
గురు - శిష్యుల నంగ నెల్ల కొమ్మలు కాగా
గురువును గానగ జాలరు
ధర లోపల మనుజు లెల్ల ; తలపరు, వేమా. ౧౭౯

గురుడ నగా పరమాత్ముడు
పరగంగా శిష్యుడ నగ పటు జీవుడ గుఱ
గురు - శిష్య - జీవ - సంపద
గురు తరముగ గూర్చు నతడు, గురువగు, వేమా.

లోకములకు గురువు, లోకులకును గురు,
వదియు దెలిసి 'మోక్ష'మందరోరి
గురుని గనక నరక కూపము బొందిరి. వి. ౧౮౧

179. The teacher is the root of all ; the disciples of a teacher are the branches* : men can seldom discern the *really excellent* teacher in the world.

180. The great spirit is our instructor ; the intelligent living creature is the learner : he is the real teacher who duly applies to each other the qualities of the preceptor and learner.

181. Know him who is the teacher of the worlds and the instructor of the people; hereby shall ye attain release (*mocsha*) : by not looking to the teacher, they have fallen into the pit of hell.

* I have ventured to substitute కొమ్మలు కాగా for the common reading కొంచెంబటే which gives no clear sense.

జీవి లోనను'ండు స్థిరమును గానక,
తిరుగున' స్థిరంబు, వరుస నమ్మి,
స్థిరము నస్థిరమును దెలియ జీవికి ముక్తి. వి. ౧౮౨

గతము జూతమ'ంటె, కల గన్న యర్థంబు;
నడుచు కాలమే'మి నమ్మ రాదు
క్షణము లోని బ్రతుకు సంసార - విభ్రాంతి. వి. ౧౮౩

తాన నంగనే' వరు తన - వార' న నెవరు
తెలిసి తెలియ లేకు, తిక్కనరులు!
అరిది పిసిని - కాయ పురుగు పద్ధతి గాఁగ! వి. ౧౮౪

182. Unable to perceive the immortality *of the soul that is* within the living *body*, he wanders, trusting to that which is unstable; our final happiness (mucti) depends on knowing what is eternal and what is temporal.

183. If I say "Let me view the past," it is like a thing seen in a dream: neither can I rely on the time now passing: our attachment to our earthly connections lives but for a moment.

184. What mean we by "self," or "our own people"? knowing, they know not, the madmen! *they live* like a *silk* worm in a cocoon, *seemingly secure, but in reality helpless.*

భయము సుమీ యజ్ఞానము
భయము డిగిన నిశ్చయంబు పరమార్థంబౌ;
లయము సుమీ యీ దేహము
జయము సుమీ జీవుడనుచు, జాటర వేమా. ౧౮౫
చచ్చె చచ్చెననుచు చావుకు వగచెదు
దీన - నరుల వెర్రి దెలుప రాదు
ప్రాణమునకు మృత్యు - బంధంబులుండునా ? వి.
జనన మరణములకు సరి స్వతంత్రుడు గాడు
మొదల కర్త గాడు, తుదను గాడు
నడుమ కర్త ననుట నగుబాటు కాదొకో ! వి. ౧౮౭

---

185. Lo, all fear is ignorance : when fear leaves us, the divine spirit shall become our own: surely* this body is perishable ; proclaim, O Vema, that the living soul *alone* shall be victorious.

186. He grieves for death, crying, "He is dead ! He is dead !" the folly of miserable men cannot be told : what, is the soul subject to the bonds of death ?†

187. Neither in his birth or at his death is he free ; he is the disposer ‡ neither of his origin or his end. Is it not ridiculous to talk of lordship in his intermediate life ?

---

* సుమీ or సుమ్మీ with జుమీ and జుమ్మీ are contracted for చూడుమీ the imperative of చూచు to see: the plural is సుండీ for చూడండి, *behold ye*; equivalent with *verily* or *surely*. *Perishable* and *victorious* might be more literally translated *perishability* and *victory*.

† The ordinary reading is ప్రాణికెక్కడి మృతి, బంధంబులూడెనా.

‡ *Carta*, a lord, agent, or disposer, signifies the responsible person on whom a matter rests ; one who has authority : Matt. vii. 29 : in the tale of Saranga Dhara, the verse "ధనఋణంబుల కర్త తనయుండు కాడె" must be translated "Is not a son the *person chiefly concerned in* our gains and losses."

బ్రహ్మమే' డద' నుచు, పలుమారు నాడేరు,
వెర్రి మూర్ఖ - జనుల విధము ఁజూడ ;
బ్రహ్మమ' న్నిట ందు, పరిపూర్ణ మై యుండు. వి.౧౮౮
పసుల - వన్నె వేరు పాలెల్లనొ' క్కటి ;
పుష్ప - జాతి వేరు, పూజ యొకటి ;
దర్శనంబు వేరు, దైవంబు * యొక్కటి. వి. ౧౮౯
పని తొడవులు వేరు, బంగారమొ' క్కటి
పరగ ఘటలు వేరు ప్రాణమొ' కటి
యరయ తిండ్లు వేరు,† యాకలి యొక్కటి. వి.౧౯౦
కాన లేదు నుదురు' కర్ణముల్, వీపున,
నెరులు గాన లేదు నెత్తిమీద,
తన్ను గాన లేదు తత్వమే'మె' రుగును ? వి. ౧౯౧

188. Mad and idiotic are those who perpetually enquiring where the deity resides : God dwells in all things in his complete fulness.‡

189. Kine are of divers colors, but all milk is alike ; the species of flowers vary, yet all worship * is one ; systems of faith are different, but the deity is one.

190. Worked chasings are various, but all gold is the same ; these *earthly* tenements vary, but the soul is one ; viands are many, but hunger is always the same.

191. We cannot see our own forehead, our ears, or our backs ; neither can we know the hairs of our head ; if a man knows not himself, how should he know (tatwam) the deity ?

---

* In which flowers are always used. † Here the elision is omitted

‡ Lives in all life, extends through all extent,
Spreads undivided, animates unspent.

The whole of this passage, in Pope's Essay on Man, conveys the precise ideas entertained regarding the deity, or ruling spirt, by those who hold the Vedanti creed.

తిఱిగి తిఱిగి నరుఁడు మఱలుకొనుటె' గాక,
నందు వలననే' మి యాస లేదు;
అంతరా - త్మ నిల్పు నతఁడె పో బ్రహ్మంబు! వి. ౧౯౨
చిత్తమ' నెడు వేరు శిథిలమై' నప్పుడె
ప్రకృతి యనెడు చెట్టు పడును పిదప,
కోర్కుల నెడు పెద్ద కొమ్మలె' ండును గదా. వి. ౧౯౩
తిట్టి కొట్టికేని తిరిగి మాఱా' డక,
నూఁరకున్నఁ జూడను' ర్వి మీఁద,
వాఁడె' గు పరమాత్మ' వర్ణింప శక్యమా? వి. ౧౯౪
కల్మషంబు పోక కనిపించదె' ందును,
రూపమె' వ్వరికిని గూఢ తోఁడ;
తామసంబు' డిగిన, దగఁ గల్గు జ్ఞానంబు. వి. ౧౯౫

---

192. A man roams and rambles, and turns back unsatisfied; he has therein obtained nothing his heart desires; he who has fixed *unalterably* his inmost heart, go to, he is the divinity.

193. When the mind, which is the root, decays, the tree of *our mortal* nature falls; then are its great boughs, the affections, dried up.*

194. He who, though reviled or struck, returns it not but remaineth unagitated; behold, on earth he is already become the great spirit; can we fitly describe his perfections?

195. Unless impurity be removed, to no one can the *divine* image become truly visible; when passion leaves thee, wisdom shall be thine.

---

* Some copies add ము కిబయలు మెరసి మొనయు, వేమ.

నీటి లోని వ్రాత, నిలువక యున్న' ట్లు
పాటి జగతి లేము, పరము లేదు ;
మాట మాటకె' ల్ల మనసు గోరుచు' నుండు ? వి.

దొంగ తెలివి చేత, దొరుకునా మోక్షంబు ?
చేత ఁగాని పనుల ఁజేయ రాదు ;
గురుడ' నంగ వలదు, గుణ హీనుడ' నవలె. వి. ౧౯౭

ఆశల ఁదెగఁ గోసి యనలంబు చల్లార్చి,
గోచి బిగియ ఁబెట్టి కోపము' డచి ;
గుట్టు మీరు వాడు గురువుకు గురువు రా. వి. ౧౯౮

ఆశల' నెడు త్రాళ్ల నమర గోయుగ జేసి,
పార వైవ గాని పరము లేదు
కొక్కు తిండి యాస చిక్కి చచ్చిన యట్లు. వి. ౧౯౯

---

196. Like as what is written in water remains not, so are all the blessings of this life unstable : why does the empty *heart* desire word upon word ?

197. Can salvation be attained by him who is false-hearted ? labour not in works that are fruitless ; the fool that thus acts shall never be called a teacher.

198. He who has cut off his desires, who has quenched the fire *of passion*, who has bound up his loins, and crushed all anger ; he who has attained to the great secret is the teacher of teachers.

199. Unless thou cut away the cords of desire and cast them off, there is no heaven for thee ; thou shalt perish like a mole ensnared by the love of food.

చెవులు గోరును మంచి జిలిబిలి పాటల,
తియ్యని మాటల తెరగు వినగ
చర్మంబు గోరును సరవి తోడుత శీత
మృదుల సంస్పర్శ సంపదలనె పుడు
కన్నులు గోరును కమనీయ వర్ణంబు
లై' నట్టి రూపంబుల నువు తోడ
నాలుక గోరును, నయము తోడుత, తీపి,
యొఁగరు, కారమ్ము, చేదు' ప్పు, పులుసు,
ముక్కు గోరును సద్గంధములను జెలఁగి,
చెవులు చర్మంబు కన్నులు, జిహ్వ ముక్కు,
నిన్నియును గూడినటువంటి యిల్లు రోసి,
తన్ను గనుగొని సుఖియింప దగును వేమ. ౨౦౦

200. The ears delight in gentle harmonious songs and sweet words well ordered : the skin in like manner is gratified by coolness and soft touches : the eyes desire forms adorned with lovely hues and delicately proportioned : the tongue naturally is pleased with *tastes* astringent, pungent, bitter, salt, and acid : and the nose takes pleasure in grateful scents. But let us abhor the *corporeal* mansion that renders us subject to the five feelings perceived by the ears, skin, eyes, tongue, and nose. See that thou art a being distinct from these earthly ties : and thus shalt thou be happy, O Vema !

END OF BOOK I.

వేమనపద్యములు

ద్వితీయభాగము.

సూక్ష్మ - రూపమెఱిగి, సుఖమొందగా లేక
బహుళముగనుఁ జదువుఁ బడుచు నరుడు ;
చావు చేటెఱుగని చదువేల చదువడో ?
విశ్వదాభిరామవినర వేమ.

ఉత్తముని కడుపున నోగు జన్మించిన
వాడు చెరుచు వాని వంశమెల్ల ;
చెఱకు వెన్ను పుట్టి చెరచదా తీపెల్ల ? వి.

BOOK II.

1. A young man who is unable to see the recondite form *of God* can enjoy no comfort, but studies excessively; why does he study that which would teach him how to die.

2. If a wicked son is born from the womb of the excellent, he will destory his entire race; as *an empty* ear growing on a sugarcane destroys all its sweetness.

తనువు యెవరి సొమ్ము తనద'ని పోషింప?
ధనము యెవరి సొమ్ము దాచు కొనగ?
ప్రాణమె'వరి సొమ్ము పాయకు'ండగ నిల్ప? వి. ౩

జీవుఁ జంపుటె'ల్ల శివభక్తి దప్పుట,
జీవున'రసి చూడ శివుడు గాడె?
జీవుడు శివుడ'నుచు, సిద్ధంబు తెలియరో? వి. ౪

పరగ చెట్ట - బట్టి పాలింపకు'ండెనా,
వెలుగ దాటి వీడు వెళ్ల బారు,
ఆడువారి చిత్తమ'టువలెను'ండు రా. వి. ౫

---

3. To whom does your body belong which you nourish so carefully? whose is your wealth that you should hide it? to whom does the soul appertain that it should not leave the body. *

4. All killing of animals is a sin against Siva: consider all animals as forms of the deity; indeed every living creature *if sinless* is as a god. †

5. If after marrying her you do not treat her with kindness, she will cross the fence and run off down the street: such is the temper of women. ‡

---

* In another MS. the third line is equivalent with the first, *viz.* బొంది యెవరి సొమ్ము పోకుండ నిల్పను. In the first two lines there are two errors in elision.

† See note on I, 126.

‡ Verses containing illiberal notions regarding the female sex are but too frequent in Vema and other Hindu authors. See on this subject Colebrooke's Digest of Hindu Law.

కొంకణంబు ఁబోవ, కుక్క సింహాము గాదు,
కాశి ఁబోవ పంది గజము గాదు,
వేరె జాతి వాడు విప్రుడు గాడ' య్యా. వి. ౬

ఇచ్చు వాని యొద్దనీ, ని వాడు' ండిన,
చచ్చు గాని యీవి సాగనీ' డు ;
కల్పతరువు కింద, గచ్చ చెట్టు' న్నట్లు. వి. ౭

అల్ప - బుద్ధి వానిక' ధికారమి' చ్చిన,
దొడ్డ వారినె' ల్లఁ దొలగ గొట్టు ;
చెప్పు దిన్న కుక్క చెరుకు తీపె' రుగునా ? వి. ౮

---

6. Though he roam to Concan,* no dog will turn into a lion; going to Benares* will make no pig an elephant; and no pilgrimage will make a saint† of one whose nature is different.

7. If a covetous man ‡ dwell near the liberal, he will die rather than endure to see his benevolence; as the thorn bush perishes if planted near the tree of desire.§

8. If authority be given to a low-minded man, he will chase away all the honorable; can a dog that gnaws shoes taste the sweetness of the sugar-cane?

---

* Two holy cities.
† *Vipra*, generally translated a Bramin. See on *Dwija*, Book I., 154.
‡ Lit. The *no-giver*.
§ The wishing tree that grows in paradise.

ఆపదందుఁ జూడుమూ' రయ బంధుల
భయము వేళఁ జూడు బంటు గుణము
పేద పడ్డ వెనుక, పెండ్లాము గతిఁ జూడు! వి. ౯

మగడు మదనుఁడై' న, మంచి కాపురమై' న,
సహజమే' ల మాను, జారకాంత?
పాలు ద్రావు కుక్క బడిబడి పోవదా? వి. ౧౦

పురుషుఁడె' రుగఁ జంపు, భూపతి విన, ఁజేటు!
అఖిల నిందకె' ల్లనా లయంబు,
పర - పురుష - గమనము ప్రత్యక్ష - నరకంబు! వి.౧౧

---

9. In adversity observe well the behaviour of your relations: in the time of fear observe the worth of your soldier; and when you fall into poverty, look well to your wife's steps.*

10. Though her husband be Cupid himself, and her home be agreeable, how shall the slippery-*footed* woman change her nature? Though a dog *be tamed* and reared with milk, will it not still rove from place to place?

11. "If my husband knows it, he will kill me: if the king hears it, it will be terrible." To go *astray* with a strange man is the greatest† of infamy: it is hell open before her eyes.

---

* The second and third lines I have corrected, both in sense and metre, from the old reading.

చూడు భయము వేళ జూడు బంటు
పేదరికమున గను, పెండ్లామె జాడల, వి.

† Lit. The home or abode of shame.

ఆలి వంచ లేక యధమత్వమునను'ండి,
వెనక వంతున'నుట వెర్రితనము;
చెట్టు ముదరనిచ్చి, చిదిమిన ఁబోవునా? వి. ౧౨
యెలుగు తోలు దెచ్చి, యెందాక నుతికిన,
నలుపు గాక నేల తెలుపు ఁగల్గు?
కొయ్య బొమ్మ ఁదెచ్చి, కొట్టితే గుణియౌనె? వి.౧౩
కుక్క తోక దెచ్చి, గొట్టంబు జేర్చిన?
క్రోవి చెంతను'ండు కొంత దడవు
యెంత జెప్ప చెడుగు పంతంబు మానునా?* వి.౧౪
ఆలు మగని మాటక'డ్డంబు వచ్చెనా?
యాలు గాదు వాని వ్రాలు గాని
యట్టి యాలు విడిచి యడవిను'ండుట మేలు! వి.౧౫

12. If through the baseness of your spirit you fail to subdue your wife *in the first instance*, it is vain to think of afterwards governing her. If you let a tree grow up, will it move for a pinch?

13. If you take a bear-skin and wash it ever so long, will it, instead of its native blackness, ever become white? If you beat a wooden image will it hence acquire any good quality?

14. If you take a dog's tail and put it into a *bambu* tube, it will remain straight but for a while; say what you will, a bad man will not lose his crooked disposition!

15. Has the wife opposed her lord's commands? she is no longer his mate but his fate.† To such a wife, dwelling in a wilderness is preferable.

---

* In another copy the third line is.
క్రోవి తీయ వెనక కొంకర్లు పోవునా?

† A play upon words is intended in the original.

మాట వినని యాలు మగనికి మృతియాను *
యోర పడగ సర్ప మొంటి గ్రహము ;
తనకు గాని యాలు దానవు రాలయా! వి. ౧౬
ఓజ మాలు పొలతి యోలి మాడల చేటు,
పోటు కోడలు బంటు కూటి చేటు;
పనికి మాలు తొత్తు బత్తెంబు చేటు రా! వి. ౧౭
తప్పులెన్ను వారు తండోపతండము ;
ఉర్వి జనులకెల్లను ండు తప్పు ;
తప్పు లెన్ను వారు తమ తప్పు లెఱుగరు. వి. ౧౮
ముచ్చు యాత్రఁ బోయి ముల్లె విడుచుగాని,
మ్రొక్క - పొద్దు లేదు మొనసి యెపుడు ;
కుక్క యిల్లుఁ జొచ్చి, కుండలు మోసునా ? వి. ౧౯

16. A disobedient wife is as *the goddess* Death to her husband ; springing hooded serpent ; a very demon ; a wife at enmity with you is a fit wife for a demon ?

17. *Upon* a wife devoid of consideration † the money of the dowry is wasted : if a soldier will not meet the battle, his subsistence is thrown away, and board is wasted on an unprofitable wench.

18. There are crowds upon crowds of those who reckon the faults of others : yet every one in the world has his failings. Those who look to the faults of others are often ignorant of their own.

19. A thief, if he goes to a holy place, will only pick the pockets of the comers ; he has no leisure to draw near and bow *to the god.* If a dog enters a house, will he tend the hearth ?

---

* Other manuscripts read మగనికి మగరాలు and మగనికి మరుగాలు.

† O'za appears to be from yochana.

కల్లలా'డు వాని గ్రామ - కర్త యెరుంగు;
సత్యమా'డు వాని, సామి యెరుగు:
పెక్కు తిండిపోతు పెండ్లామె'రుంగు రా; వి. ౨౦

పాగ, పచ్చడంబు; పైకి కూసంబును,
పోగులు, 'ంగరములు, బొజ్జ కడుపు,
గలిగిన'ట్టు వాని ఁగందురు చుట్టాలు. వి. ౨౧

ఈత కం'టె లోతునె'ంచగ పని లేదు;
చావు కంటె కీడు జగతి లేదు;
గోచి పాతకం'టె, కొంచెంబు మరి లేదు. వి. ౨౨

జాణలైన యట్టి చపలాయతా'క్షుల,
వలపుల'రసి చూచి, భ్రమయనే'ల?
బయలి రూపులె'ల్ల పరికింపగానే'ల? వి. ౨౩

---

20. He that is a liar is known to the lord of the village : the lord knows him who speaks the truth : but the vile glutton is known to his *wretched* wife alone.

21. A turban, a quilted dress, and a fine coat,* necklaces, rings, and a fair round belly. He that has these virtues is looked to by all his kin.

22. If you know how to swim, there is no necessity to sound *the stream* : if you know how to die, there is no grief in world *from which suicide will not release you.* If you *are content with* a girdle, no poverty *will distress you.*

23. Why, at viewing the charms of the roguish swimming eye, do we become enamoured of its light? why should we so delight to view all external beauty?

---

* For "pai ki cusambunu," which also means a snake's skin; some ead "paicambu saneulu," or bags of money.

ఇంతి జూచెనేని, నింతంత యన రాదు,
కాల వహ్ని లక్క గరగిన' ట్లు
వట్టి మోహమి' ట్లు రట్టుల జేసె రా! వి. ౨౪
కలిమి గలిగెనే' ని కాముగా జూతురు,
లేమి చేత జిక్కి, లేవ లేని
మదను వంటి వాని మాలగా జూతురు! వి. ౨౫
కలిగిన మనుజుండు కాముడు సోముడు
మిగుల తేజమునను మెరయుచు' ండు
విత్త-హీనుడె' ంత రిత్తమై పోవును! వి. ౨౬
విటుల కనులకె' ంత విభ్రమమై' యుండు,
సాటి లేని పొలతి చక్కదనము
కంటిలోని పాప కుంటెన గాడయా. వి. ౨౭

24. When he beholds a woman, he is deprived of power to estimate her justly; and is consumed *with love* as resin would be in the hottest fire: into what follies are we led by empty desire!

25. If one be possessed of wealth, they look upon him as the god of love: but if he falls into poverty, and is unable to rise *and help himself*, be he Cupid himself they look upon him as a Pariar.

26. The man of wealth is *considered fair* as Cupid or the *regent of* the moon; he shines illustrious by his possessions but if he loses his riches, how vile he becomes!

27. How strong a charm cast on the eye of the lover is the form of a matchless beauty: surely the pupil of her eye is the go-between!

గురువునకును పుచ్చ కూరై న నివ్వరు,
అరయ వేశ్యకిత్తు రర్థమెల్ల
గురుడు వేశ్య కన్న కులహీనుడే మకో? వి. ౨౮

తీపి లోన తీపి తెలియంగ ప్రాణంబు
ప్రాణ వితతి కన్న పసిడి తీపి;
పసిడికన్న మిగుల పడతి మాటలు తీపి. వి. ౨౯

పనస తొలల కన్న పంచదారల కన్న
జుంటి తేనె కన్న జున్ను కన్న
చెరుకు రసము కన్న చెలి మాట తీపిరా! వి. ౩౦

కొమ్మ దిమ్మరై న దిమ్మరులకు వల్చు;
సరస విటులకేల సమ్మతించు?
పేడ ఁజిన్న పురుగు బెల్లమే మెరుగురా? వి. ౩౧

---

28. To the teacher they will not give even a mess of stale food; but on a courtezan they will bestow their whole wealth: ah! is the doctor more degraded than the dancer?

29. What is dearest † of all things? life: but gold is dearer than a thousand lives: and dearer than gold are the words of a maiden.

30. Sweeter than the core of the jack-fruit, than refined sugar, than the honeycomb, than thick cream, ‡ and than the juice of the sugar-cane; sweeter than all these are the words of a beloved damsel.

31. A woman who is a rover loves none but rovers: how should she be pleased with a delicate lover? The dung-bettle cares not for the sweetness of sugar.

---

* Dus-sandhi. † Lit. Sweetest.

‡ Lit. Beestings, the first milk given by a cow after bearing a calf.

ఆలి వంక వారలాత్మ బంధువులైరి;
తల్లి వంక వారు తగిన పాటి;
తండ్రి వంక వారు దాయాది శత్రువూ. వి. 3౨

కుక్క యేమి యెరుగు గురులింగ-జంగంబు?
పిక్క యొడసి పట్టి పీకు గాక
సంత పాక తొత్తు సన్యాసి నెరుగునా. వి. 33

తొత్తు తోటి పొందు తొర్రి పెసల మూట
ముచ్చు తోటి పొందు వచ్చు నింద
తలవరింటి పొందు తలతోటి దీరురా? వి. 3౪

---

32. Your connections on your wife's side or your most intimate relations; those of your mother's kin are but so and so; but your connections on your father's side belong to the side of your enemies.*

33. Will a dog recognize the linga zangam † priest; it will only snap at him, seize, and tear the calf of his leg. And equally little does the prostitute who lives in a booth at a fair care for the *saintly* palmer.

34. Intimacy with a callet ‡ is like a hole in a bag of grain; connection with a rogue leads to infamy; and to associate with bailiffs will be paid for with your head.

---

* Dayadi, paternal relations: here used for "enemies." We find the same idea in Latin attached to the term *patruus*. In some copies the first line is thus, neglecting the requisite elision ఆలి వంక వారు యాప్త బంధువుల్.

† A class of the priests of Siva. Several verses in this author appear like this one, to have orginated in some casual occurrence that the poet happened to witness.

‡ See Shakespeare, Othello, Act iv., Scene 2. The word also occurs in Chaucer; and I use it rather than more common modern synonyms.

తనదు నృపతి తోడ తన యాయుధము తోడ,
నగ్ని తోడ, పరుల యాలి తోడ,
హాస్యమాడు టెల్ల, ప్రాణాంతమౌ సుమ్ము. వి.
మంచి రుచుల గోరు మంచి స్త్రీలను గోరు,
మనుజుడెంత చెడ్డ మనసు జూడ;
యించుకంత యైన నేలని విడువడు. వి. ౩౬
తరుణి సొగసు గన్న తనయుల గన్నను,
మరుని కళల మించి మనము బారు;
పాప - జాతి మనము బట్టంగ రాద యా! వి. ౩౭

---

35. If you sport with your prince, with weapons, with fire, or with a strange woman; this will lead to destruction! *

36. He desires pleasant food, and he longs for fair women! behold the evil heart of man! He † cannot for an instant relinquish these *temptations* and reflect that they are unprofitable.

37. Gazing on the beauty of his wife and on his sons the affection ‡ of love increases, and his heart runs on them. How difficult is it to curb the sinful mind!

---

* In other copies పరస మాడుకెల్ల బ్రాణాంతకంబు.

† Lit. He cannot even in the least say Why these?

‡ Cala. A word used in many different senses: which however, may, I think, be all resolved into "degree, grade, shade, tint." It is particularly applied to degree of light, whereby the moonlight of one night differs from that of the next: applied to the mind it denotes feeling or affection; to natural objects, the effect or AFFECTION produced on one body by another. In mystic philosophy, Vemana and other authors seem to use the term for feelings that affect the nerves. It is there used in conjunction with two other words: [illegible] and [illegible]; the

తేనె, పంచదార, తియ్య మామిడి పండు,
తిన్న గాని తీపి తెలియ రాదు;
కన్నసింపు - బుట్టు ఁగామిని యధరంబు! వి. ౩౮

ఎద్దుకన్న దున్న యేలాగు తక్కువ?
మెఱుపు లేకపోయి తరిగె విలువ *
నేర్పెరుగని వాని నెర యోగి యందురా? † వి

---

38. Whether it be honey, sugar, or a luscious mango, unless we taste it sweetness is not perceived; but at merely seeing the lip of a lovely maid, we feel its sweetness.

39. In what respect *is it that* buffalo is so inferior to the ox; what is its price lower because it is not red *but black*? Then let no one be called wise who is devoid of understanding : *his intrinsic value alone should be considered.*

---

three terms thus signify ideas received through the *ears*, the *eyes*, and the *feelings* of the body. Thus among the erotic works, the Cala-sastra is a *Treatise on Feelings*; the humour or disposition of the body being imagined to vary daily.

In Telugu Grammar the term Cala is applied to sixteen classes of words, the last of which is very dubious." The reason for using this title is given in none of the grammars, but I imagine it is borrowed from the *calas* or phases (so to call them) of the moon of which fourteen are reckoned in each lunar fortnight, while the fifteenth is considered apart, being either new or full moon. In my opinion the *Cala* in the grammar are all easily reducible to four or five classes instead of sixteen.

* In most copies this line stands thus, iluva being, for the sake of rhyme, put for the viluva—

మెఱుపు లేక పోయి యిలువ దరిగె

Were we to write విలువ the rhyme would be defective, as is explained in Prosody under the title Akhanda yati అఖండయతి.

† Here అందురా is for అనుదురా.

పదుగురాడు మాట పాటియై ధరఁజెల్లు
నొక్కఁడాడు మాట యెక్కఁదెందు;
నూరకాడు - వానికూరెల్ల నోపదో* వి. ౪౦

గుణ - యుతునకు వేరు గోరంతఁజేసిన,
కొండ యౌను వాని గుణము చేత;
కొండ కొద్ది మేలు గుణహీను డెరుగునా. వి. ౪౧

పతిని విడువ రాదు, పదివేలకైనను,
పెట్టి చెప్ప రాదు, పేదకైన;
పతినిఁదిట్ట రాదు, సతి రూపవతియైన. వి. ౪౨

---

40. What ten men affirm passes current in the world: is the assertion of a single witness ever valued? the whole town detests the mere *interminable* talker.

41. If you do the smallest † service to a worthy man, his worth makes it *in his eyes* a mountain *of benefits*: but will the unworthy acknowledge even the heaviest obligations?

42. Desert not the king even for a thousand ‡ *others:* when you have given a man food, tell it not however poor you are; and however fair the wife be, let her not scorn, her husband. §

---

* In general written నూరకుండు వానికూరెల్ల నోపదో.

† Lit. A nail-full.

‡ A common intensive phrase.

§ The second line might also be interpreted "however poor he be;" the carelessness of style in this writer often leaves passages thus doubtful, and has led to the erroneous idea entertained among the natives that his verses are all riddles, conveying a different meaning from that which appears.

సుతులు సతులు మాయ; సుఖ దుఃఖములు మాయ;
సంసృతియును మాయ జాలి మాయ *
మాయ బ్రతుకుకి' ంత మాయ గప్పి' స్తివి! వి. ౪౩

మాట నిలుప లేని మనుజుండు చండాలు
డా' జ్ఞ లేని రాజు ‡ యాండు ముండ
మహిమ లేని వేల్పు మంట (జేసిన పులి! వి. ౪౪

---

43. Sons and wives are a mere delusion; pleasure and pain are a deception; a family and affections we feel are unreal: thou hast filled this delusive life with empty forms.†

44. The man who cannot keep his word is *vile as* a pariar; a king dovoid of authority is as a lone widow women; and a god not acknowledged in the land is no better then a clay *image of a* tiger.

---

* This I conjecture must have been what the poet wrote. The verse occurs only in one manuscript, and there the line stands thus.

సంసరణము మాయ, జాల్వ మాయ.

Where జాల్వ would seem contracted for జాళువా gold, a word that does not admit of such a change.

† *Maya*, "*Unreal*; because things which are always changing have no real existence. The doctrine of Plato, who calls God TO " "ON, and describes material things as scarcely really existing." (Stillingfleet on Paradise Lost, x, 471.) Thus the *Param-A'tma*, or Great Spirit, is described as "That which supremely *exists*." (Compare Exodus, iii., 14).

‡ Dus-sandhi.

సిగ్గు వారలమ' ని సృష్టి లోపలి వారు
వెఱ్ఱి వేమని గని వెరగు పడిరి;
తనకు గలుగు సిగ్గు దైవమె'రుంగురా! వి. ౪౫

విడువ ముడువ లేక, కుడువ కట్టగ లేక;
వెరపు లేక, విద్యనా' రయు లేక;
వెడల లేని వాని నడు పీనుగం దురో. వి. ౪౬

లేని కాలమునకు, లేని మనమునా', ందు;
యీనిన పులి రీతి నె' రుగకు' ండు
కఠిన బుద్ధికి, ట్లు కలిమే' మి గల్గురా. వి. ౪౭

---

45. Those who consider themselves decent *and reputable* look upon the mad* Vemana with astonishment; ah, the deity knows his *real humility while he appears only to deride others*!

46. He who can neither loose nor close *his purse*; who will neither feed nor clothe himself; devoid of genius and un-polished by learning; he who thus walks is like a walking corpse.

47. In time of povery the heart itself becomes poor, and senseless as a cubbed tigress; † how should any good accrue to one so base-minded?

---

* Vemana has, in many passages, called himself a madman, with a view, we may suppose, to securing himself from the vengeance he was likely to incur by his unsparing satires on Hinduism and the Braminical hierarchy. Thus, also, Lucian Rabelais assumed the garb of fools and madmen while the arguments conveyed in their writings were undermining the polytheistical systems of their times. Erasmus, too, in his book entitled *Laus Stultitiæ*, has adopted this method with a like object.

† Which is imagined to lose sight and sense, and even to devour its cubs.

ఇంచుక ' ంత బోనమీ ' శ్వరా ' ర్పణము ' న్న,
పుణ్య లోకమునకు (బోవున' తడు *
అన్న దానమునకు నధిక దానము లేదు. వి. ౪౮

ప్రియము లేని విందు పిండి - వంటల చేటు,
భక్తిలేని పూజ, పత్రి చేటు,
పాత్ర మె' రుగనీ' వి' † బంగారు చేటురా. వి. ౪౯

తన్ను తా న' రుగడు తా న' వ్వరికి నేర్పు?
పాలుమాలి తిరుగు పశువు కొడుకు!
కాసుల కొరకై తె కర్మముల్ (గట్టురా! వి. ౫౦

---

48. If he offer ever so little of his meal to the Lord, he shall go to the blessed abodes ‡ *in heaven.* Thus no charity is superior to that of bestowing food.

49. A feast given without kindness is a mere waste of flour-cakes; worship devoid of piety is a waste of the sprouts *used in sacrifice*; § and gifts devoid of charity are a mere waste of gold.

50. Being ignorant of himself, how shall he instruct others? he roams about idly, no better than a brute, ¶ and performs religious ceremonies for the sake of pitiful fees.

---

* Dus-sandhi

† ప్రా పిలే నియ్యావి in another MS.

‡ Punya. Blessed or holy. Holy acts are explained to be those which cause actual merit in the performer; they are thus distinguished from *Dharman* (already explained), which confers no *merit,* but to omit which is sinful: while *punyam* is that which is voluntary or spontaneous, without any immediate hope of reward: being a work of *supererogation*, or which is gratuitous and uncalled for. In this sense it is even applied to evil acts. (Campare note on *Carmam*, v. 51.)

§ See note on I, 189.

¶ For పశువు one copy has పనస. The sense of the third line is not clear.

సుతుల చేత పుణ్య - సుఖము బొందుదమ' ని,
మనుజుడు' ండు కర్మ - మతము దగిలి ;
యేనుగు పడి యున్న నె', త్తునా మశకంబు ? వి

ఎంత చదువు ఁజదివి యె', న్ని విన్ననుగాని,
హీనుడ' వగుణంబు మాన లేడు
బొగ్గు పాల గడుగ, ఁబోవునా మలినంబు ? వి. ౫౨

మొదల తన మతము వదలక,
తుదనె వ్వరి మతమునై' న దూషింపకయుఁ,
ఁబదిలుడ' యి, కోర్కిఁ గోరక,
ముదమున జరియించు వాఁడె, ముఖ్యుడు వేమా !

---

51. Imagining that by acquiring some he will attain the happiness that is the reward of merit, * a man remains entangled in the creed of works. If an elephant fall into a pit, how can a gnat extricate it?

52. Let him study what he will, or listen *to the holy texts*, the sinner will not relinquish his vile nature. Though you wash a coal in milk, will its blackness be removed?

53. He who, in the first place, swerves not from his own religion; who in the second place, reviles the creed of no other man who cautiously refrains from forming any *evil* desire: he shall live in happiness: he is the first of men.

---

* See note on II, 48, on *Punyam* here opposed to *Carmam*, which forms the lowest grade in the scale of merit. See the proceeding verses.

తిర్రి వాని మిగుల దీవించగా రాదు,
వెర్రి వాని మాట వినగ రాదు,
వెర్రి కుక్కఁ బట్టి వేటాడ వచ్చునా ? వి. ౫౪

ఆలు బిడ్డలు, ధనమ' రయ తల్లియుఁదండ్రి,
కై,* మనుజుడు మిగుల కష్ట - పడును
తనకు నెవరు లేరు, తాను బ్రహ్మము గన్న. వి. ౫౫

పూస పోగులై' న పుట్టంబు, విడియంబు,
కాయ - పుష్టి మిగుల గలిగి యున్న,
హీన జాతినైననీ' ందు రమ్మ' ందురు. వి. ౫౬

మాసిన పని తోడ, మలిన - వస్త్రము తోడ,
యొడలజిడ్డు తోడను' ండెనే' ని
యుగ్ర' - జన్ముడైన, బొ పొమ్మ' ందురు. వి. ౫౭

54. Why utter benedictions on a worthless wretch? why listen to the words of a fool? who can pursue the chase with mad dogs?

55. A man labors to gain wealth for the sake of his wife, his child, his mother, and his father. But if he looked to God, these should no longer exist *so as to agitate him.*

56. If they see a man wearing beads, earrings, and a vest with a roll of betel, and plumpness of body, be his caste what it may, they invite him to *sit by* them.†

57. But if unshaven, with soiled garments and a foul body, *like a hermit,* be his birth what it may, they bid him begone.

---

* The Syntax is here imperfect.

† Campare verse 21. Sometimes in this author we meet (as in Martial and the Anthologia) with the same epigram in different forms; and it is not always easy to decide which the poet ultimatly preferred.

కొండెగాఁడు జావ కొంప దనుక బోవ్వ,
వంతు కొంతె కాని, వగపు లేదు
కొంకనక్కఁ జావ గొఱ్ఱెలేమిటికేడ్చు? వి.* ౫౮
వాడకురికి తిట్టు, వలదన్న మొఱఁ బెట్టు;
ముందు మగనిఁ దిట్టు ముసుగుఁ బెట్టు;
గడుసురాలు మగని గంప బెట్టమ్మురా. వి. ౫౯
ఆస పాప-జాతి యన్నిటికంటెను
ఆస చేత యతులు మోస పోరె
చూచి విడుచు వారు శుద్ధాత్ములెందును. వి. ౬౦
నిజములాడు వాని నిందించుజగమెల్ల
నిజములాడరాదు నీచు తోను
నిజ-మహాత్ముగూడి నిజమాడ వలయురా. వి. ౬౧

---

58. When a backbiter dies, you should go *to the funeral at* his house, but merely for decency's sake: it is impossible to grieve in reality: can the sheep lament the death of the wolf?

59. She runs rangling down the street: if you check her; she screams, she first scolds her husband, *and then* hides her face *in a fury:* the shrew is ready to sell her husband in a basket.

60. Covetousness is a sin of the worst nature: through lust have not even hermits been deluded? he who hath viewed and relinquished all this is the pure spirit!

61. He who speaks *rough plain* truth is reproached by all the world. Truth should not be declared to the vile; but if you meet with a truly great soul, declare the truth to him.

---

* In the original తోడెలొట్టిచావతో గొఱ్ఱె యేడ్చునా, a line in every point wrong; here todelu becomes a dactyl. I have, therefore, corrected it from conjecture.

వెరువ వలె పాపమునకును,
వెరువగ వలె మరణమునకు, విశ్వము లోనఁ
మరువగ వలె సంగమముల,
మరి మరువగ వలదు మేలు, మహిలో వేమా. ౬౨

ఇచ్చకము భువిని వశ్యము *
కుచ్చితమీ లోక నింద కోవిదునకునీ,
తుచ్ఛమున, హాని వచ్చును;
మచ్చరమే తన్నుఁ జెరుచు, మహిలో వేమా. ౬౩

కోతిఁ బట్టి తెచ్చి, కొత్త పుట్టము గట్టి †
కొండముచ్చులెల్ల గొలిచినట్లు,
నీతి హీనులొద్ద నిర్భాగ్యులుండురు. వి. ౬౪

---

62. Let us fear to sin and stand in awe of death. Let us forget the ties of earthly affections; but never let us forget kindness *that we have received.*

63. Civility is indispensable in the world, but hypocrisy is a disgrace to the most sagacious *of men*: baseness leads to ruin, and malice towards others leads to our own destruction.‡

64. If you catch a monkey and dress it in a new robe, the hill apes will all worship it. Thus are the luckless subject to the senseless.

---

* This would more correctly be thus ఇచ్చకము వశ్య-కరమగు, but in the original it is ఇచ్చకము లోకవశ్యము.

† *Al.* (కొండ పట్టము గట్టి) "constitute it king of the hills."

‡ Maccaram appears to be derived from the Sanscrit *matsaram.* The prasa in the third line is not accurate.

గాడ్దె మేను నిండ గంధంబు బూసిన
యేమి యెరుగ లేక యెగసి తన్ను
నీడు కాని దానికి' ష్టమీ' లాగు, రా.   వి.
విడువ వలయునూ' రు విశ్రాంతి గాకున్న,
విడువ వలయునా' లి విధము దెలిసి
విడువ వలయు రాజు వితరణి గాకున్న.   వి.
అప్పు దీయ రోత హరి హరాదులకై' న *
మొప్పె తోడ మైత్రి మొదలె రోత
తప్పుఁ బలుక రోత తాకట్టి' డిన రోత   వి.
ఎడ్డె దెలుప వచ్చు యేడాదికైనను,
మౌనిఁ దెలుప వచ్చు మార్గమునను;
మొప్పె దెలుపరాదు ముప్పదే' ండ్లకునై' న.   వి.

---

65. Though you anoint an ass all over with perfumes, it feels not *your fondness*, but will turn again and kick you: and equally fruitless is love shown to a young girl.

66. You should go from a town where you are not at ease; quit a wife whose temper you have found out and leave a prince who is devoid of liberality.

67. To fall in debts is vile even to the noblest: intimacy with fools is an utter abomination: a lie is disgusting; and to give a pledge is intolerable. †

68. A blockhead may be taught in a year's time; a silent recluse may be led in the path; but an idiot can never be instructed, no, not by thirty year's teaching.

---

* Lit. "To Hari, Hara, and the rest;" that is, "to Vishnu, Siva, &c."

† The word *rota*, vile, is here translated in four different ways; as the reiteration of the same word is not in English approved as it is in Telugu.

చూలు * వలన బుట్టుసుఖ దుఃఖములు రెండు;
పతికి సతికి బుట్టు పరగ సుతుడు
సతికి సుతుని వలన సౌఖ్యంబు గలుగును. వి. ౬౯

నీళ్ల మీఁద ఁజూడు నెరయు నోడల పర్వు;
బయలు మీఁద ఁజూడు పక్షి పర్వు;
నాడు వారి గమనమా' లాగు నుండు రా. వి. ౭౦

ఆలు రంభయైనన' తి శీల వతియైన,
జార - పురుషుడే' ల జాడ మాను?
మాల వాడ కుక్క మరగిన చందంబు, వి. ౭౧

---

69. From our offspring originate both pleasure and pain; the son is born equally of the husband and the wife; and the wife derives comfort from the son.

70. Like the course of ships on the sea; like the course of a bird in the sky; such is the conduct of a woman that leaves no traces behind it.†

71. Be his wife Venus, and full of fidelity, how shall the fickle husband cease from his habit *of rambling*; he is like a dog that delights only to roam the Pariar-street.

---

* I have substituted చూలు for చూపు which would seem an error of the transcriber.

† Compare Proverbs, xxx. 19. Another copy reads in the second and third lines.

బట్ట బయలు జూడు బండిలి మి
ఆడదాని బలిమి యాడనె చూడ రా

చాకి వాఁడు కోక చీకాకు - పడఁ జేసి,
మయిలఁ బుచ్చి మంచి మడుపుఁ జేయు,
బుద్ధిఁ జెప్పు వాఁడు గుద్దిన నే' మయా? వి. ౭౨
కలిమినాఁడు మగని కామిని చూచును,
లేమిఁ జిక్కు నాఁడు లేవదు' ండు
మనిన మగని నై'న మడియుంగఁ జూచును. * వి. ౭౩
పాలు పంచదార పాపర పండ్ల లో
జాలఁ బోసి వండ చవికి రాదు
కుటిల మానవునకు గుణ మే' ల కలుగురా. వి. ౭౪
భూమి నాది యన్న భూమి పక్కున నవ్వు
దాన హీనుఁ జూచి ధనము నవ్వు†
కదన భీతుఁ జూచి కాలుండు నవ్వును. వి. ౭౫

72. The washerman torments a cloth to take the stains out, and then folds it properly; what then though he who teaches thee chastise thee.

73. In the time of his wealth the wife looks *with kindness* on her husband; when he falls into poverty she will not *even* rise *to meet him:* she looks then upon her living husband as though dead.

74. Though you pour milk and sugar over bramble berries and boil them, they will acquire no flavour; how then can *good* qualities be produced in the crooked heart *by any kindness*.

75. If he says this ground is my own, the field laughs at him. His wealth derides *the miser* who never bestows a gift! and death ‡ laughs at him who is afraid in battle.

* మడియుంగ. In some copies మాయును, and మాలవానిగచూచు.

† Al. ధనము నాది యన్న ధనము నవ్వు. ‡ Cala is Time or Destiny.

తనదు భ్రాతలె' ల్ల దానంబు సేయంగ,
తనకు గలద టంచు' మనగ రాదు;
తనదు కాలు నోయ, తన తమ్ముడే' డ్చునా? § వి.

పంకజా' క్షి (గన్న బంగరు పొడగన్న,
దిమ్ము బట్టి యుండు తెలివి కెల్ల; *
మనుజులకును తత్వ మహిమె' ట్లు గల్గురా? వి. ౭౭

---

76. If your elder brothers by charity become doers of good do not suppose that the reward of this will accrue to you; the younger brother might as well feel a wound inflicted on the elder.

77. When we behold a bright-eyed† girl, or gaze on gold every one's mind is seized with wavering *thoughts*; how then can the power of truth ‡ be felt by men?

---

§ In another copy a more apt expression is introduced by sacrificing metre.

తన యన్న కాల్గోయ తన కాలు నొచ్చునా.

* For తెలివికెల్ల some copies read బొమ్మకైన, or బమ్మకైన (derived from Bramha), while others have తమ్ముకైన. Possibly the allusion to Bramins is what the poet intended; as the Hindu authors constantly represent their gods as subject to every human passion. In such passages the name Bramha may well be translated as Jupiter.

† Lit. *Lotus-eyed*; allusions to the lotus (padma)' or water-lily, perpetually occur in the Sanscrit and Telugu authors. In their poetical use we may always translate the *pundaricam*, or white species, as *the lily* and the red lotus, or *ken-damara*, as *the rose*, a flower apparently little known to the poets of India. The *utpalam*, or blue lotus, may thus be rendered *the violet*.

‡ Tatwam. See on 1, 137.

దాతఁగాని వాని తరుచుగా వేడిన,
వాడు దాత యౌనె వసుధ లోన?
నెపురు దర్భ యౌనె యబ్ధిలో ముంచిన? వి. ౭౮

మొండి వానికేల ముంజేతి కడియాలు?
తొఱ్ఱి వానికేల కఱ్ఱ పండ్లు?
గాడిదెలకునేల గడ్డముల్ మీసముల్? వి. ౭౯

దొడ్డ వాండ్లమనుచు, దోవ డొంకలు కట్టి,
యడ్డమైన జనుల నంటఁ గట్టి; *
దోచుకొన్న నట్టి దోషమెక్కడ బోవు? వి. ౮౦

---

78. However importunately you pray *relief* of an illiberalman, will he ever become bountiful? Will plunging *them* in *sacred* sea convert bulrushes into darbha-grass?†

79. What has a criple to do with bracelets? of what advantage are wooden teeth to the harelipped? will an ass be the better for *assuming* a beard and whiskers? *Mere pretensions are wholly fruitless.*

80. You think yourselves brave men when you obstruct a road with bushes, bind the people who come up, *and pluuder them*: how shall the guilt of robbery be removed from you?

---

* Al. అడ్డమైన పనుల నంటగట్టు
దొడ్డిపెట్టినట్టి ద్రోహమెక్కడబోవు!

† Which is used in sacrifice.

పట్ట నేర్చుపాము పడగ యోరగ ఁజేసు;
చెరుప ఁజూచు వాడు చెలిమి ఁజేసు ;
చంప ఁదలచు రాజు చనువి'చ్చుచు'ండు, రా. వి. ౮౧
ఎంత సేవ ఁజేసి యేపాటు ఁబడినను,
రాచ మూఁక నమ్మ రాదు ర'న్న ?
పాము తోఁటి పొందు పది వేలకైనను ? వి. ౮౨
మొదల క్రియను ఁదప్పి మోసంబు ఁజేసుక,
పొట్టకొఱకు మనసు పొందు పరచి
బీదకుక్క రీతి పెరుగును మనుజుండు. వి. ౮౩
కడు విచిత్రమ'రయ కాముని యంత్రంబు ; *
పువ్వుబోఁడి చుక్క బొట్టు ఁగన్న ;
కాంచి - వెళుకు † గన్న కడు సౌఖ్య పుట్టురా. వి.

---

81. A serpent when ready to strike sidles its crest: he who seeks to destroy you contracts friendship with you; and the prince who meditates your destruction allows you every freedom.

82. Whatever obedience you use, whatever toil you undergo for them, never, O my brother, trust the assembly of kings ; it is always‡ *hazardous as* intimacy with a serpent would be.

83. He who neglects the highest end *of his being*, practises guile, and who restrains his inclinations merely for the sake of his belley, such a man lives like a miserable dog.

84. Singularly fancitul is the talisman of Cupid to behold ; the spot § in *the forehead of* the rosy nymph ; at the glance of her waist is the heart agitated.

---

* Al. కామినియంగంబు. † Al. కాంచనంబు.

‡ Lit. For ten thousand ; a common intensive. See on II, 12.

§ The *tilaca*, or beauty spot ; an ornamental patch worn in the forehead.

చక్కెర గలుపుకతింటే
ముక్కిన తవుడైన లెస్స; మోహము గలచో
వెక్కురు బానిసె * యైనను
మక్కువతో దివ్య భామ; మహిలో వేమా. ౮౫

ఎట్టి వానికైనఁ బుట్టును మోహంబు,
పుట్టు మోహమెల్ల పూడ ద్రొక్కి,
గట్టి చేసి చూడ, గనిపించు బ్రహ్మంబు. వి. ౮౬

పట్టు గొమ్మ లేక బహుపాటుఁ బడు వారు
పెట్టి పొయ్య లేక పెట్టు వారు,
ముట్టి శివుని పూజ మొదలె సేయగరాదు. వి. ౮౭

35. If you mix sugar with it, even mouldy chaff *has flavour*; so wherever there is inclination, the most unpalatable hussy is loved as a divine angel.

86. Love is produced in *the heart of every man* whomsoever; but if thou bury and trample upon desire *whenever it is* produced, and restrain it, then, behold, the deity shall be displayed to thee.

87. Those *on the one hand* who are without sustenance and suffer distress; and those *on the other* who will give neither meat nor drink, but only revile others; are equally incapable of performing the worship of Siva.

---

* Al. కక్కురపు బానిసె which gives a similar sense.

ఆత్మలోన శివునిన' నువుగా శోధించి,
నిశ్చలముగ భక్తి నిలిపెనేని,
సర్వ - ముక్తుడౌ'ను సర్వంబు తానౌ'ను. వి. ౮౮
ఎరిగిన శివ - పూజ యెన్నడు చెడి పోదు,
మొదల బట్టు పట్టు వదల రాదు,
మొదల విడిచి గోడ తుది ఁబెట్ట ఁగల్గునా? వి. ౮౯
చేటు వచ్చెనేని చెడనాడు దైవంబు,
మేలు వచ్చె నేని మెచ్చు ఁదన్ను,
చేటు మేలు తలప చేసిన కర్మము. * వి. ౯౦
కడుపు చిచ్చుచేత, కామా' నలము చేత,
క్రోధ - వహ్ని చేత కుటిల పడక,
నొక్క మనసు తోడను' ండిన' ప్పుడె ముక్తి. వి. ౯౧

---

88. He who seeks aright the God who dwells in the heart, and fixes unalterable faith on him, he shall attain utter absorption; he shall be resolved into the universe.†

89. Worship of God, performed according to knowledge, shall never perish *fruitless;* never let *a man* leave the hold he first takes ; can a wall be completed if the foundation be neglected ?

90. If misfortune befall him, *the sinner* reviles the deity: if he meets with good, he lauds himself for it : but evil and good are the *result of his own* acts.

91 Be not ensnared by the fire of hunger, by the flame of desire, or the heat of anger. If thou maintain one changeless disposition, this is freedom. ‡

---

* Al. గరిమ మేలు కీడు కావటి కుండలా.

†On *Siva,* see I., 133. n. On *mucti,* see I., 88, n. On *Sarvam,* I., 171, n.
‡ *Mucti.* Liberty. See verse 94.

ఏవంక మనసు కలిగిన
నావంకకుని'ంద్రియంబుల'న్నియు నేగుఁ ;
నీవంక మనసు గలిగిన
నేవంకకుని'ంద్రియంబులే'గవు, వేమా. ౯౨

పాలు పెరుగు వెన్న * పాయసాన్నము నెయ్యి
జున్ను నెన్నియైనఁ జూడ పాలు
పాలవంటి కులము † బ్రహ్మంబు గానరో. వి. ౯3

చదువులందు రాజ్య - పదవులందును, పాడి
మొదవులందు, స్త్రీల పెదవులందు
నా'శలు'డుగున'ట్టి యయ్యలు ముక్తులు. వి. ౯౪

---

92. Whatever be the inclination of the heart, to that side do all the senses turn ; if the heart be once turned to Thee, the passions will never wander in any other direction.

93. Plain milk, or curds; butter, or rice-milk; *neyi* ‡ or beestings ; however many *shapes it may assume*, it is still milk; men cannot perceive *that* the deity is thus *also capable of various appearances.*

94. Those who no longer delight in reading, in royal mansions, in milch kine, and in the lips of women—these venerable men ¶ are the free.

---

* Al. చల్ల. † Al. గుణము.

‡ Clarified butter, called in Hindustani *ghee*.

¶ *Ayya*, Sir. A father or master. A wife calls her husband *Swami*, my lord, but never *Ayya*.

కడుపు కేల మనస కళవళ పడియెదు
కడుపు కేడ తృప్తి కలుగుచుండు ?
కడుపు రాతిలోని కప్పకు గలుగదా ? వి. ౯౫

శూద్రుతనముపోయె, శూద్రుడ గానని,
ద్విజుడనుకొనుటెల్ల తెలివి లేమి *
ఇత్తడగు పసిడి యీడన వచ్చునా ? వి. ౯౬

అధికమైన యజ్ఞమెల్లను తాఁజేసి,
మొనసి శాస్త్రము విడి మురువు దక్క
దొబ్బ నేర్చు కుక్క దుత్తలు మోసునా ? వి. ౯౭

---

95. Why suffer anxiety, O my heart, for the belly? either here or there the belly will be filled. As to having a belly, the frog that lives in a rock is thy equal.

96. To say, "Sudraism has left me, I am no Sudra, I am a Bramin,"† is all folly; though brass resemble gold, can it be esteemed its equal?

97. If a light man perform the dignified *yagna* sacrifice, departing from the prescribed rule, he shall miss the enjoyment *of good*; a dog will merely push down the cup it attempts to lift.

---

* Substituted for తెలివి లేక.

† The sons of Bramins are considered to be by birth Sudras: the ceremony of *upanayanam* or *initiation*, performed at about six years old, confers the name of Dwija, or Twice Born.

జన్మనా జాయతే శూద్రః, కర్మణా జాయతే ద్విజః,
వేదాధ్యాయీచ విప్రః స్యాత్, బ్రహ్మజ్ఞానీచ బ్రాహ్మణః.

"By birth he is a Sudra: by religious rites he becomes a Dwija; by reading the (Veda) Scripture, a (Vipra) perfect priest; and, by a knowledge of rahma, a (Brahman) divine.

శాంత మానసమున జల్లనై శీతల,
భాతిను' న్న వాడు పరమ - యోగి
యట్టి వాడు ముక్తిన' తి వేగ గైకొను. వి. ౯౮
కనకమొ' డల, మంచి కాంతల యెడలను,
వలచి యుందురె' ంత వారలై' న
తోయ జాక్షిఁ బాయు దొరలె' వ్వరును లేరు. వి. ౯౯
మధు - రసంబు గోరి, మక్షికంబులు చేరి
చొచ్చి వెడల లేక చొక్కిన' ట్లు,
మునిగి వెడల లేడు మోహంబు రాశిలో. వి. ౧౦౦
ఒడలుఁ బెంచు లంజె యుబ్బసంబునై' న,
వేగ, విటుని మీద విరిగనే' ని
పందికొక్కు మీద, బండి గల్ * పడ్డట్లు. వి. ౧౦౧

---

98. The man of calm mind, whose disposition is benign as a cool *temperature*, he is the perfect Yogi. Such a man shall very soon attain *to holy* liberty.

99. All men, be they who they will, desire gold and fine women. Not the mightiest of lords can relinquish a fair-eyed † maiden.

100. Like flies that longing for honey, approach it, enter, are intoxicated, and unable to extricate themselves: so, plunged in a multitude of passions, a sinner perishes without escape.

101. If a prostitute with a well-nourished body, and puffed up, suddenly fall on a paramour, rushing on him, he perishes like a dormouse under the wheel of a cart."

---

* కల్ for కల్లు. A stone. The wheels of carts are sometimes formed of stone.

† Lotus eyed. See on

వెలయాలి వలన కూరిమి
కలుగదు, మరి, కలిగనే ని, కడతేరదు రా
పలుగురు నడిచెడు తెరువున,
పులు* మొలవదు ; మొలిచనే ని పొదలదు ; వేమా.

తొత్తు తోటి పొందు దోషంబు దోషంబు ;
లంజె తోటి పొందు లజ్జ చెడును:
జార తోటి పొందు చావుకు మూలమా. వి. ౧౦౩

బ్రహ్మమున్న చోటు పరగంగఁ దెలియక,
యెందు వెదుక బ్రహ్మమే ల కలుగు ?
నంజనంబు లేక నా సొమ్ము దొరకదు ? వి. ౧౦౪

---

102. She who sells herself has no real affection for you; or, should she have any, it will not last. In a path trodden by many no grass will grow; or, should it spring, it will never thrive.

103. To associate with a slut is ruin upon ruin; he who has to do with a whore, loses all shame; and joining with an adulteress is the source of utter death.

104. If we know not truly the abode of the deity, how should we discover it, search as we may? that object cannot be traced without the *requisite divining* rod. †

---

* పులు for పుల్లు.

† *Anjanam.* A spell, or more properly a collyrium; a salve which, applied to the eyes, was supposed to give the power of discovering mines or buried treasures. It is alluded to by Milton, *Paradise Lost* xii., 415.

వెర్రి ముద్దుకే' ల వేద శాస్త్రంబులు?
ముద్దులాడికే' ల ముసలి మగడు?
సద్ది మిగులని' ంట సంసారమే' ల రా? వి. ౧౦౫

సాధు చరిత యైన, సతి సత్ప్రవర్తన,
జార యేమె' రుంగు సాధువైన?
బ్రహ్మ నిష్ఠ' మెరుగు (ప్రాకృతుడె' రుగునా? వి. ౧౦౬

హీనుడె' న్ని విద్యలి' లన' భ్యసించిన,
ఘనుడు గాడు, హీన - జనుడె కాని
పరిమళముల గర్ధభము మోయ ఘనమౌనె? వి.

చక్కదనములే' ల, సంపత్కరములే' ల,
విద్యలే' ల' భూమి విరివి యేల?
పుత్ర - పదవికన్న పుట్టునా పదవులు? వి. ౧౦౮

---

105. What has a stupid fool to do with an old husband? and what sort of family is that where nothing is kept *for the morrow*?*

106. As the inconstant woman comprehends not the faithful wife's virtuous conduct; so the natural man cannot understand steadfastness in religion, when he sees it.

107. Though the man of base heart have learnt all the sciences in the world, he does not *thereby* become noble, but is a depraved being. Will rubbing perfumes over an ass, at all alter its nature?

108. To what ends is gracefulness of form, or the acquisition of riches, or *the knowledge of* arts, or extent of landed *possessions*? Can any gain equal that of having offspring?

---

* Lit: for breakfast సద్ది being probably contracted for చలిది; cold food prepared the preceding day and eaten in the morning by children before the regular hour at which grown persons eat.

భాగ్యవంతురాలు పరుల యాఁకలి దప్పి,
ఁదెలిసి, పెట్ట నేర్చు' ఁదీర్చ నేర్చు,
తనదు దుష్ట-భార్య తన యాఁకలిని గాని *
పరుల యాఁకలె' రుగద' రయ వేమ. ౧౦౯

మనసు లోనను' న్న మమతల' న్నియు ఁగోసి,
దృఢము జేసి మనసు ఁదేట పరచి,
ఘటము నిల్పు వాఁడు, ఘతనర-యోగిరా. వి. ౧౧౦

పచ్చ విల్తుచేత గ్రచ్చర జనులె' ల్ల
తచ్చునా' డ బడిరి ధరణి లోన,
కులజుఁడె' వ్వఁడి' ందుఁ గుల-హీనుఁడె' వ్వఁడు? వి.

కాగల పనులె' ల్లఁ గాకె' టు బోవును !
కాని పనులు కానె కావు భువిని,
మహిమ వేరె యుండ మనతోడను' న్నదా ? వి.౧౧౨

---

109. A lucky woman perceives the hunger and thirst of others; she helps them *to food* and satisfies them; but your unlucky, senseless wife considers no one's hunger but her own.

110. He who understands all the secrets of his heart, who has cut off his passions and purified himself; he who restrains his body, this is the true saint.

111. By *Cupid*, the green-bowed *god*, are all men in the world suddenly deluded; who, then, *in this respect* is the noble, who is the abject?

112. How should all that is destined to happen fail of occurring? that which is not doomed to us shall never befall us? The *ruling* power is independent of ourselves.†

---

* Al. తనదు దుష్ట భాగ్య తనయాఁకలిని గాని.

† A paraphrase of a verse difficult to translate literally, but useful as exemplifying various forms of the verb *agu* to *become*.

శత్రువులను ద్రుంచి, శాంతంబు వహియించి,
కృత్యములను నడపు నిత్యునె’ రిగి,
సత్యమ’ ణగకుండ *సాధించిన’ టువంటి
పురుషుడో’ ను పుణ్య పరుడు వేమ! ౧౧౩

తనదు దేహమందు తనకు’ న్న పరివార
మ’ ందరి ‹బిలిపించి, హర్షమె’ సగ,
నెల్ల చావు దెలిసి, యింద’ ందునె’ రిగియు
నడువ నేర్చునా’ తడ’ రుదు వేమ! ౧౧౪

మొదటనా’ స ‹బెట్టి, తుద "లేదు పొమ్మ" న
పరమ లోభులై’ న పాపులకును ;
వారి యుసురు దాకి వగ చెడి పోవరా? వి. ౧౧౫

---

113. He who has quelled his foes, *the passions* ; who has put on patience ; who recognizes the eternal agent in all that happens : and without failing in the truth, has attained *to it* : this man shall become a holy saint.

114. He who willingly summons *the passions*, his servants in the body ; who knows they shall all *perish in* death ; who knows this world and the next : † he who thus walks is rarely to be found.

115. Those who first excite hopes *in the poor*, and at last say "Go, I have nothing for you ;" those sinners, the hard misers, shall ultimately feel the effect of the sighs‡ of men, shall lose their hopes and perish.

---

* Al. అడగకుండ which gives the same sense. The fourth line is commonly thus పురుషు డుండు పుణ్య భూమి వేమ.

† *Indu. Andu* answering to the Sanskrit *Iham* and *Param*, literally signifying *here* and *there* ; but imply the *present* and a *future* world.

‡ B. 1., 44.

బడుగున' రుగ లేని ప్రాభవంబ' ది యేల ?
ప్రోది యుడనిబంధు - భూతి యేల?
వ్యాధిఁ దెలియ లేని వైద్యుఁడు మరి యేల ? వి.

తుంట వింటి వాని తూఁపుల ఘాతకు
మింట మంట నడుమ మిడుకఁ దరమె?
యింటి యాలు విడిచి, యెట్లు' ండ వచ్చురా. వి.

పాముకన్న లేదు * పాపిష్ఠ మ'గు జీవి
యట్టి పాము ఁజెప్పిన' ట్లు వినును ;
[యిలను] మోహిఁ దెల్పనె' వ్వరి వశమయా. వి.

---

116. To what end is wealth if unknown to the poor? of what profit is the prosperity of a relation who shows no liberality? and of what good is a physician unknown to the sick?

117. There is no living between earth and sky for the pain of the wounds inflicted by Cupid. † How can a man live who deserts the wife of his home?

118. No animal is more vile than the serpent, yet the serpent will obey that which is said to it; but in whose power is it to teach mildness to the lustful man?

---

* In the original the verse stood thus, with an error in elision పాపిష్ఠ జీవము యట్టి, &c. In several other passages I have made similar conjectural emendations without pointing them out to the reader.

† Lit. *Him of the sugar cane bow.*

ఎవ్వరె' రుగకు' ండనె' ప్పుడు బోవునో?
పోవు జీవము' ట్ల బొంది విడిచి,
యంత మాత్రమునకున' పకీర్తినె' రుగక,
విరగ బడును నరుడు వెర్రి వేమ? ౧౧౯

తనువు విడిచి తాను తర్లి పోయెడు వేళ,
తనదు భార్య సుతులు తగిన వార
లొ' క్కరైననే గరు' సురు మాత్రమె కాని,
తనదు మంచి తోడు తనకు, వేమ. ౧౨౦

పూర్వ వాసన గల పుణ్యా-త్ముని కలిమి
యూట చెలమ రీతి నూరునెప్పు
డె' ందరికిని సంగనె' ప్పటి యట్లు' ండు. వి. ౧౨౧

---

119. This soul * will depart; it will pass away, and leave the body one day or other unknown to any one: he is a madman who, unconscious of the degradation he shall meet *in death*, is puffed up *with pride*.

120. When he quits the body and departs, neither his wife, sons, nor connections will one of them follow him nothing but the soul † will then remain; and the good he has done will be his only possession.

121. The wealth of him who is virtuous, and retain a consciousness of his former birth, shall flow *continually* like a wellspring. To how many soever he gives, he shall still remain *wealthy*.

---

* *Jivi* is properly the living *body*. Perhaps the poet wrote *bratucu*.

‡ Lit, breath, *usuru*.

ఆడి తప్పు వారల' భిమాన హీనులు
గోడు' రుగని వాడు, కొద్ది కాడు,
కూడి కీడు సేయు క్రూరుండు ఁదలపోయు. వి. ౧౨౨
వాన రాకడ మరి ప్రాణంబు పోకడ
కాన ఁబడదు ఘనున కై' న గాని
కాన ఁబడిన మీద కలి యిట్లు నడుచునా. వి. ౧౨౩
తగిన కులజుడై' న, తల యెత్తు ధనమైన,
భాగ్య - పురుషుడే' ల పట్టనే' ంచు
పరమ - సాధ్వి చూడ, పరులన' ంటదు సుమీ. వి.
పరుల దత్తమి' ట్లు పాలన జేసిన,
నిల స్వ దత్తమునకుని' నుమడించు
నవని పరుల దత్తమ' పహరించిన స్వద
త్తంబు నిష్ఫలంబు ; ధరణి వేమ. ౧౨౫

---

122. Those who give their word, and break it, are lost to all shame : he who disregards distress is vile: and cruel is he who, after contracting friendship, grieves his friend.

123. The coming of rain and the departing of the spirit are not to be foreseen even by the wisest. Could we perceive *the future*, surely this iron age (Cali yuga) would not proceed as it does.

124. Though he see wealth heaped as high as his head, the man of pure birth,* rich in himself, will not touch it; and a chaste, virtuous wife will regard no strange man.

125. If thou duly guard the benefaction of others, *thy ancestors, such as charitable institutions*, this shall double the merit of thy own charities: but if thou embezzle the alms of others, thy own charities shall become fruitless.

---

* Or, The fortunate man.

తనదు దానమ' వని తన కూతురి సమంబు,
తండ్రి దానమె' ల్ల దనకు తోడు
అన్యులి' చ్చు దానమ' ది తల్లి వంటిది* వి. ౧౨౬
గతము చేసిన' ట్టి కర్మబంధముల' న్ని,
పరిసి పోవు, సత్య - గురుని వలన;
కుమ్మరికొ' క యేడు, గుదియకు, నొకనాడు† వి.
జాతుల'ందు మిగుల జాతి యేదె' క్కువో?
యెరుక లేక తిరుగనే' మి ఫలము?
యెరుక గలుగు వాడె, హెచ్చైన కులజుండు. వి.

---

126. Consider the gift made by thyself, *such as endowments for charitable uses, granted in life time*, as thy daughter: thy father's bequests, as thy sister; and those of thy elder brother, as thy mother.

127. All the bonds wherewith our former actions, *in an earlier transmigration*, have bound us, shall be done away by a teacher of the truth; *as they say* "a year to a potter and a day to a cudgel." ‡

128. Which is the chief caste among all the sects? What is the use of going on without sense?§ He who has understanding is of the noblest tribe.

---

* Borrowed from the Sanskrit verse.

స్వదత్తా పుత్రికా ధాత్రీ, పితృ - దత్తా సహోదరీ.
అన్య - దత్తా స్వయం మాతా, విప్ర - దత్తా - వసుంధర.

† Al. నొకవేత a single blow.

‡ Which can easily destroy his year's work. Some copies for nadu read pettu, *a blow*.

§ Here, as in many other prosaic passages, fidelity of translation requires the use of very unpoetical (gramya) language.

కూటికి వగ లేక కూర్చున్న' వారికి,
నా'డు దాని మీఁది యాస గలదె?
యన్న - మదము చేతన'న్ని మదంబులౌ. వి.

అన్ని జాడలు' డిగి యానంద కాముడై
నిన్ను నమ్మ జాలు, నిష్ఠ తోడ,
నిన్ను నమ్ము ముక్తి నిక్కంబు, నీయాన. వి. ౧౩౦

ఒడ్డు పొడుగుఁ గలిగి, గడ్డంబు పొడుగైన,
దాన - గుణము లేక దాత యగునె?
యెనుము గొప్పదై'న, యేనుగుఁ బోలునా? వి.

సతుల జూచి, నరుడు సౌఖ్యంబు గోరును;
గతుల గాన లేడు, కర్మమందు
గతుల సతుల వలన గానంగ లేరయా. వి. ౧౩౨

---

129. Can they who have no means of subsistence feel any desire for women? All our lusts originate in fulness of meat.*

130. He who gives up every other object, and, seeking happiness alone, trusts in Thee with full reliance; by that faith shall (I protest by Thee) gain perfection.

131. Be he stout or tall, or wearing a long beard, devoid of liberality he is no noble: however large a buffalo be, it cannot compare with an elephant.

132. Looking on women, a man desires happiness, but cannot foresee what will thereby befall him; by reason of women they are blinded to their destiny.†

---

* See I., 12.

† Or, To salvation: *gati* being equivalent to *mocsham*.

ఆలి మాటలు విని, యన్న దమ్ముల రోసి,
వేరు బడెడు వాడు, వెర్రి వాడు;
కుక్క తోకఁ బట్టి గోదావరి దునా; వి. ౧౩౩

స్త్రీలు గల్గు చోట, చెల్లాటములు* గల్గు;
స్త్రీలు లేని చోటు చిన్నబోవు;
స్త్రీలచేత నరులు చిక్కుచు న్నారయా. వి. ౧౩౪

మాల మాల గాదు, మహి మీదనే' ప్రొద్దు;
మాట తిరుగు వాడు మాల గాక;
వాని మాల యన్న - వాడై (పో) పెను మాల. వి.

చిప్ప లోను బడ్డ చినుకు ముత్యంబా' యె
నీళ్లఁ బడ్డ చినుకు నీళ్ల గలసె;
ప్రాప్తము గల చోట ఫలమే' ల తప్పునో?† వి.

---

133. He is a fool who, listening to his *fractious* wife, quits his brothers and separates himself *from them*. Can a man swim in the Godavery by holding on to a dog's tail?

134. Where there are women, there is sport: the town would be ruined but for women; men are indeed in the hands ‡ of women.

135. Consider not him a Pariar *of degraded rank* who is so by birth; he who breaks his word is far viler. He who reproaches the Pariar is (go to) worse than him.

136. The drop that falls into the oyster-shell becomes a pearl, while the drop that falls into the wave turns to water: if the situation be suitable, the fruit shall not fail.

---

* In another M S. బిందు లోన పడ్డ బిడ్డడు పుట్టిదా.

† Al. కొరకు for చేత. ‡ Al. చెల్లాటం.

కులముఁ గలుగు వారు, గోత్రంబుఁ గలవారు,
విద్యచేత విఱ్ఱవీగు వారు,
పసిడి గల్గు వాని బానిస కొడుకులు. వి. ౧౩౭

కాని వాని తోటి కలసి వర్తించెనా
హాని వచ్చునెంత వానికైన,
తాటి క్రింద పాలు తాగిన చందమా. వి. ౧౩౮

కరగ కరగఁ బుట్టు కనకంబునకు వన్నె;
పెనగ పెనగ బుట్టు ప్రేమ సతికి;
ముదియ ముదియఁ బుట్టు మోహంబు, లోభంబు. వి.

ఎరుక లేని దొరల నెన్నాళ్లు గొలిచిన,
బ్రతుకు లేదు, వట్టి భ్రాంతి గాని
గొడ్డుటావు పాలు గోరితే చేపునా? వి. ౧౪౦

---

137. Men of *pure* caste, and of high descent, and those who overflow with learning, are *after all esteemed less than* the sons of the handmaid of the rich man.

138. If he joins himself to the vile, and associates with him, he will be ruined, whoever he be. It is like drinking milk under a palm-tree.*

139. By melting and fusing, the huge of fine gold is produced; by embracing and clasping, is love produced in a woman; and as we grow older and older, cupidity and avarice are produced.

140. However long you serve a prince void of sense *you will gain* no living, but mere expectations: if you stroke a dry cow's udder, will it produce milk?

---

* Where, however innocently, it would be suspected he was drinking wine. Some copies read యాగకడుపు చొచ్చి యుట్టట్టు సేయఁబా.

గొడ్డుటావు (బితుక కుండ గొంపోయిన,
పండ్లునూడ (దన్ను పాలు లేవు,
లోభి వానిన' డుగ లాభంబు లే' దయా. వి. ౧౪౧

కులము లేని వాడు, కలిమిచే వెలయును;
కలిమి లేని వాని' కులము దిగును;
కులము' కన్న మిగుల కలిమి ప్రధానంబు. వి. ౧౪౨

నెయ్యి లేని కూడు, (నీయాన) కసువ' ది
కూర లేని తిండి కుక్క తిండి
ప్రియము లేని కూడు పిండపు కూడు రా! వి. ౧౪౩

---

141. If you go with a pail to milk a dry cow it may kick your teeth out, but you will get no milk. Such is all that you will gain by begging of a miser !

142. The man of no birth is still honored for his wealth and he who has nothing, sinks in caste. Thus is wealth honored above birth.

143. Rice dressed without *neyi** is, I protest to thee,† mere grass ; a dinner without herbs is only fit for dogs ; unapalatable meats are as vile as funeral oblations.

---

* See on verse 93, Book II.

† Ni ana, a form of adjuration, as in Romeo and Juliet. "Swear by thy gracious self." This phrase is supposed to come from అనుట because the swearer laid his hand on the object sworn by. In the tale of Saranga-Dhara, we meet with the word in this couplet:

ద్వి. వామాక్షి యీ దుష్ట వర్తను గావ
నా మీద యాన, నీ నయనంబులా' న.

"Cease, O lady, from these evil thoughts, by thyself, by thine eyes I adjure thee!"

నోటి పుప్పి కొల్లనొప్పి లేకుండగా
నాకు పోక సున్న మౌషధంబు
పెట్టకుండెనేని పెను రోత వేసురా! వి. ౧౪౪

అన్న - మదమువలనన తివలు నరులట్టు
లేపు రేగి, మదనుడేచెనందు
రన్నముడుగు వెనుకనతడెందుఁ బోయెరా! వి.

ఎర్రదాసివాడు నేపారఁ జూచిన,
వేకిఁ బుట్టి చాల వెర్రిఁ బట్టు,
పల్లుఁ దెరచి నగిన, బట్టు పెన్భూతంబు. వి. ౧౪౬

హీన - జాతి వానిని లు జేర నిచ్చినా
హాని వచ్చునెంత వానికైన;
యీగ కడుపుఁ జొచ్చి, యిట్టట్టుఁ జేయదా? వి.

---

144. Paun, areca, and chunam, serve as a medicine against decay of the teeth; and not to use this is very uncleanly.

145. When women and men are heated by fulness of meat, they say that they are tormented by Cupid. But when they have no food to eat, what becomes of that god's power.*

146. When we ardently behold a fair female, we feel a thrilling fever we are seized with madness; if she smiles and shows her bright teeth, the great devil seizes us.

147. If you suffer a low-minded wretch to creep into your house, you will lament it who ever you be. If a fly enter the stomach, will it not torment you?

---

* See. II., 129.

అల్పుడైన వానిక' ధికారమ' బ్బినా
దొడ్డ కొంచెమ' నక తూల, ఁబల్కు,
చెప్పు గొరుకు కుక్క చెరుకు చవే' మె' ర్గు? వి.
ఎట్టి స్త్రీల గనినని' ంతంత యన రాదు,
కాలవహ్ని లక్క గరగిన' ట్లు,
యిట్టి గాఢ మోహ మె' ంతైన జేయురా? వి. ౧౪౯
కాంత కుంకయైన కాని కులంబైన,
బాయ లేక విటుడు * భ్రమసి యుండు
మరగి గుడ్డి కుక్క మాంసంబు గన్నట్లు. వి. ౧౫౦
పప్పు లేని కూడు పరులక, సహ్యమౌ;
న' ప్పు లేని వాడె యధిక బలుడు ;
ముప్పు లేని వాడు, మొదల సుజ్ఞానుడు. వి. ౧౫౧

---

148. If a light man gain authority, he will not inquire who is worthy or not, he will overthrow all: what should the shoe-gnawing dog know of the sweetness of the sugarcane?

149. We admire all women without discrimination, who ever they be; † we melt as gum would do in the flame of destruction: this strong cupidity plunges us in unspeakable troubles.

150. Though a woman be a widow, or of a degraded tribe, her spark * doats upon her, unable to quit her, like a blind dog that pines after flesh.

151. Rice without herbs is ungrateful to the guest; one who is out of debt is *thereby* the more powerful; and he who is free from death, is the noblest of the wise.

† Lit. Whatever (qualescunque) women we see, we cannot esteem them such or such.

* Vitudu or vitaca a beau, rake or gallant; a paramour or lover; an "amoris or amoroso," words by which the Latin term *procus* is explained in Ainsworth.

పేదరికమ' ంత దోషం
బే' దో యీ జగతిలో' నవీ' శ్వరుడె' రుగున్
పేదను పొడగను వాడున్,
కాదని శవమ' నుచు జూచు : గదరా వేమా. ౧౫౨

ధార్మికునకు గాని ధర్మంబుఁ గన రాదు,
కష్ట జీవికె' ట్లు గాన బడును,
నీరుఁ జొరక లోతు నిజముగాఁ దెలియదు. వి. ౧౫౩

మొగము జూచినపుడె, మోహంబు ఘనమౌను,
ధనము * జూచినపుడె, దగులు మనసు,
కూలిన ప్పుడ, రయ కుసులెల్ల విరుగును. వి. ౧౫౪

ఎన్ని మతములై' న, నే' మంత్రమైనను,
సత్యమి' ంత లేకఁ జూడ విడదు
సత్యము గలిగు' న్న, జగతిలో' ద్విజుడ' య్యె. వి.

---

152. The misery of poverty is known to God alone. He who views the poor man and holds him as nought, is no better than a corpse.

153. A good deed is valued by the good alone: how should the vile sinner perceive its excellence? unless you enter the water (I protest to thee †) its depth cannot be known.

154. At beholding her face, love arises in the heart, at viewing money, we are ensnared; we fall *into the snare*; and all our joints are broken!

155. Be thy creed or thy prayers what they may, unless thou have a little truth thou shalt not attain the path *to happiness*. He who possesses the truth is the twice-born *saint*.‡

---

* Al. ధగము. † See on verse 143. ‡ Dwija. See on verse 96.

పరుల మోసపుచ్చి, ధర ధనమార్జించి,
కడుపు నించుకొనుట కాని పద్దు,
ఋణము సేయు మనుజు డెక్కువ కెక్కునా? వి.
స్థిరము గాని క్షుద్ర - పర - కూటములఁ జేసి,
హెచ్చు తగ్గు నొంది హీన మతులు
గాడ్దె పిల్లలగుచు గ్రక్కునఁ జెడుదురు. వి. ౧౫౭
ధర్మ మన్న వినరు, తము నమ్మి భూ - నరుల్
యముని వారు వచ్చి యడలు నించి
చొచ్చి కొట్ట తమరు చొరబార గలరొకో. వి. ౧౫౮
దానమడుగు - వాడు ధరలో నధముండు
దానమడుగఁ డేని, దైవసముడు;
దానమీని వాడె ధన్యుండు కాడయా. వి. ౧౫౯

156. To deceive your neighbour, heap up wealth, and so fill your belly, is infamous. He who is free from all debts, shall rise higher than all others in distinction.

157. The base wretch who forms criminal connections, *equally* unstable and infamous, and plays fast and loose *with others*, shall, like a young ass, suddenly be destroyed.

158. The men of the earth trust to themselves, and will listen to no *teacher of* righteousness: * but the messengers of Pluto † come, and fill them with horror, rushing upon them to destroy them: ah! how shall they escape?

159. He who sues for charity, is the lowest of men: he who refuses to ask for it, is *independent* as a god: and he who bestows nothing, is no rich man.

* Dharmam. † Yama.

తనకు ప్రాప్తి లేక, దాతలి' వ్వర' టంచు,
దోష-బుద్ధిచేత దూరు టె'ల్ల
ముక్కు వంకఁ జూచి, ముకురంబు దూరుట. వి.

పెక్కు జనులఁ జంపి, పేదల వధియించి,
డొక్క కొరకునూ' ళ్లు దొంగిలించి,
యెక్కడికిని బోవనె' రిగి-యముడుఁ జంపు. వి.

తండ్రి కన్న సుగుణి తనయుడు గల్గెనా,
పిన్న పెద్దతనము లె' న్న దగదు,
వాసుదేవు విడిచి, వసు దేవు నె' ంతురా? వి. ౧౬౨

పాలనీ' డిగి' ంట గ్రోలుచును' ండెనా,
మనుజులె' ల్ల గూడి, మద్యమ' ండ్రు,
నిలువఁ దగని చోట నిలువ నిందలు వచ్చు. వి. ౧౬౩

---

160. If by your own misfortune the patron bestows nothing on you, to revile him out of an evil heart is like abusing the mirror because it reflects your own crooked nose.

161. He who kills many men, and slays the poor, and plunders the villages to fill his belly, go where he will, Yama will find and destroy him.

162. If the son be more excellent than the father, why should we consider which is younger and which is the elder; who would esteem Vasudeva higher than *his supposed son* Crishna ?*

163. Were you to drink milk at a tavern, all would imagine it to be wine : so he who stands where he ought not, will *inevitably* incur reproach.

---

* Here called by *vriddhi,* Vasudeva. Some copies read.
వసుధ కృష్ణునివలె వసుదేవు నెంచురా.

కన్న-పుత్రునాస కనకంబు మీఁదాస,
స్త్రీల మీఁది యాస, చిత్తమొడలి,
భ్రమలు విడువకున్న, బ్రహ్మంబు గానరో? వి.
చెట్లు చేమ* గొట్టి, చుట్టు గోడల బెట్టి,
యిట్టునట్టు పెద్ద యిల్లు గట్టి,
మిట్టి పడును నరుడు మీఁది చేటెఱుగక? వి. ౧౬౫
† వచ్చేదిని పొయ్యేదిని
చచ్చేదిని గనగ లేక సహజములనుచుఁ ;
విచ్చల విడిగాఁ దిరుగుట
చిచ్చున బడినట్టి మిడుత చెలువము, వేమా. ౧౬౬

---

164. Unless thou free thy mind from the love of thy own ‡ son, or of gold, or of women, and free thyself from such delusion, thou shalt not see God.

165. After felling the trees, and walling in a spot, and building so large a house, a man is puffed up with pride ; and forgets the ruin that awaits him.

166. We reflect not on our coming and going, or on dying ; these we consider inveitable ; we rove at random ; like grasshoppers we leap into the flame.

---

* *Chema* is a mere expletive, or *anucarana*, and may be translated by "and the like" or etcetera.

† The forms of the verb here used are unpoetical, and belong to the colloquial style. We may, therefore, substitute వచ్చునదిపోవున దియును చచ్చునదియు or else వచ్చుటయునుపోవుటయును, చచ్చుటయును or else వచ్చున ?, పోవునదియును చచ్చునదియు.

‡ This expression, *canna*, prefixed to the words father, mother, son, or daughter, implies relation by blood, not by mere adoption.

ఒక్క తోలు దెచ్చి యొరపు బొమ్మను జేసి,
యాడు నట్లు జేసి, యట్టె వేసె ;
తన్ను దిప్పు వాని దానెల కానడో? వి. ౧౬౭

పర - బలంబు జూచి, ప్రాణ - రక్షణమున
కురికి పారిపోవు పిరికి నరుడు,
యముడు కుపితుడైన నడ్డమెవ్వండయా? వి.

తల్లి దండ్రి చావ, తనయుడు తానేడ్చు,
మగడు చావ నాలు వగచుచుండు,
కార్య - వశమె కాని కలుగదు మోహంబు? వి.

మనసు లోని ముక్తి మరి యొక్క చోటను
వెదుక బోవు - వాడు వెర్రి వాడు,
గొర్రె జంక బెట్టి గొల్ల వెదుకు రీతి. వి. ౧౭౦

---

167. We take a skin, and form it into an elegant puppet; we make it play, and then throw it away. But who can see Him who *that* plays with us *as puppets?*

168. When the coward beholds the enemy's army he flees to save his life. But if Yama be enraged who can oppose him?

169. When his mother or father dies, the son weeps; when the husband dies, the wife laments. This, however, is selfishness, * not real love.

170. The source of final happiness is inherent in the heart: he is a fool who seeks it elsewhere *as at holy places and pilgrimages:* he is like the shepherd who searched for the sheep which was in his bosom.

---

* *Carya vasham*, lit: Subjection to acts; participation in (good) treatment.

ఆశకన్న దుఃఖమ' తిశయంబుగ లేదు,
చూపు నిలుపకు' న్న సుఖము లేదు
మనసు నిలుపకు' న్న మరిముక్తి లేదయా. వి. ౧౭౧
తత్వ హీనులు' ండ్రు తరుచుగా భువిలోన,
తత్వమె' రుగు వారు తరుచు లేరు
కలిగి రేని వారు కన్పింప రార' యా ! వి. ౧౭౨
తాను నింద్రియముల ఁదనర జయించిన,
తత్వమ' రసి చూడ ఁదాన యగును
రాజ-యోగి యిట్లు ఁదేజరిల్లుచును' ండు. వి ౧౭౩
స్త్రీల మాయచేత ఁజిక్కి తా ఁగొన్నాళ్లు,
తగులు ఁగోరున' ట్లు దగిలి పోవు,
తనిసి పొలిసి తాను దైవంబు చేఁజెడు. వి. ౧౭౪

---

171. There is no torment greater than that of our lusts : unless thou fix thine eye upon it, thou shalt attain no ease : and unless thy heart be fixed, there is no salvation for thee.

172. Numerous are those who are ignorant of tatwam the truth ; and few are those who are aware of it : and it is difficult to perceive who they are that know it.

173. He who has truly vanquished his lusts, shall, by knowing the truth, be converted into truth. Thus shall he shine illustrious as the exalted Yogi.

174. Being for a while entangled in the delusions of women, he longs to be united to them, and is ensnared. He grows aged, and dies, and is destroyed by God.[*]

[*] The variations in the manuscripts are so numerous in this verse, that it is difficult to determine what the author intended.

చెప్పులోని రాయి, చెవులోని జోరీగ,
కంటిలోని నలుసు, కాలి ముల్లు,
నింటిలోని పోరు, నింత' ంత గాద' యా   వి. ౧౭౫
వార కాంతలె' ల్ల వలచి యేతెంతురా ?
పొందు ఁజేసి ధనము పుచ్చు కొరకు,
మారకమ్మ ఁజొచ్చి, మరి యిల్లు వెళ్లునా ?   ౧౭౬
గురము * గూడు ఁజేసి, గుణము వత్తిగ ఁజేసి,
సరవి కర్మ - సమితి ఁజమురు ఁజేసి,
మూలనొ' క్క-జ్యోతి ముట్టించి చూడరా ? వి. ౧౭౭
ఎన్ని యెన్ని పూజలె' న్ని ఁజేసిననే' మి ?
భక్తి లేని పూజ ఫలము లేదు !
భక్తి గల్గు పూజ బహుళ - కారణము రా!   వి.

---

175. A stone in the shoe, a gadfly in the ear, a mote in the eye, a thorn in the foot, and a quarrel in a family—*however small in themselves* are unspeakably tormenting.†

176. Is it through affection that courtezans draw near to men? They approach you to plunder your property. If you suffer the goddess of death to enter your house, will she again quit it?

177. Convert thy *corporeal* dwelling into a candlestick, and the properties *of thy nature* into a wick; let thy acts be instead of oil; and, finally, be illuminated with a certain *divine* flame.

178. However many modes of worship we reckon up, no adoration, devoid of faith, is of avail. Faithful homage is the only true means of attainment.

---

* Tadbhava, for గృహం and on గుఱం. see Lexicon.

† This is one of the few verses in which Vemana appears to have intended a double sense. The import is mystical, though the words are plain.

శివు - గుడిని దీపమి' డినను,
శివు మందిరమె' ల్ల వెలుగ ‹జేయుట యరుదా !
శివ - యోగి జ్ఞాన దీపము
భువనంబుల వెలుగ జే' యు, పొలుపుగ వేమా. ౧౭౯
ఆపగాలి వెంటన' దవుల వెంటను,
కొండ రాళ్ల వెంట, గొడవనే ల ?
ను, ల్లమ' ందె శివుడ' టుండుట ‹దెలియరు ! వి, ౧౮౦
లలిత - శివ - తత్వ - పథమున
గలసిన శివ - యోగి యేల గలసును జనులన్
జల బిందువు ముత్తియమై,
కలసునె తొల్లింటి నీట గనరా వేమా ? ౧౮౧
గాడ్దె' యేమె' రుంగు, గంధంబు వాసన ?
కుక్క యేమె' రుంగు గొప్ప కొద్ది ?
యల్ప డేమెరుంగు హరుని గొల్చు విరక్తి ? వి.

179. If a lamp be lighted in a temple, is it wonderful that its brightness should fill the whole dome? Thus shall the light of wisdom, shining in the heart of a saint, illuminate the whole world.

180. To what end is this toil of pilgrimages to the confluence of rivers, to holy streams, and round the rocks of the mountains? They know not that God dwells in their own body.

181. How should the holy saint, who is become united with the divine abode, again be mingled with men? When a drop of water is converted into a pearl, will it again unite with its former wave?

182. Can an ass comprehend the fragrance of perfumes? Does a dog know good from bad? Can the light fool understand the holy separation of him who serves God?

మూడు వేళలందు ముదముతో శివునా' త్మ,
పూజ సేయు - వాడు పుణ్య - మూర్తి!
పూజ లేక, మోక్ష - భోగంబు దొరుకునా ? వి.
రుద్ర - రూపుఁ దాల్చి, రుద్రుని నిందించి,
భ్రష్టు త్రోవఁ దిరుగు భ్రష్ట జనులు,
రంకుకుఁ దిరిగేటి రమణుల వలెను' ండ్రు. వి. ౧౮౪
ఒడలు బడల జేసి, యోగులమ' ను వారు †
మనసు కల్మషంబు మాన్ప లేరు,
పుట్ట మీదఁ గొట్ట భుజగంబు చచ్చునా. వి. ౧౮౫
మాల - వానిఁ జూచి యేల నిందింపంగ ?
పాటి - లేని మాట పలుకుటో' కటె,
వాని - లోనఁ బల్కు వాని కులం బే' ది ? వి. ౧౮౬

183. He who at the three times *of morn*, noon, and night, delights to worship God in spiritual adoration, he alone is absolutely holy: devoid of worship, can we attain the enjoyment of sacred freedom?

184. The fallen wretches who walk in a depraved path, who wear the form of Rudra,* and still dishonor him, are like fair women who live in adultery.

185. Those who mortify their bodies, calling themselves saints, are yet unable to cure the impurity of their hearts. If you merely destroy the outside of a white-ant hill, will the serpent *that dwells therein* perish?

186. Why should you revile a Pariar when you see him? this is merely unmannerly language. Of what caste is He who speaks in the Pariar? ‡

* A name of Siva, whose titles in most of these verses are equivalent to the name of the Supreme Being.

† Al. వొడలబన్ను కొన్న నోగుల వేషంబు.

‡ See notes on Book I., verses 171 and 183.

కుక్క యేకతంబు, కొక్కెర ధ్యానంబు,
గాడ్దె రాగమె,' న్నఁ గప్ప మునుగు ?
ఆత్మ నె' రుగు * భావమ' దియే లఁ జేయరో. వి

సకల శాస్త్రములను ఁజదివియు వ్రాసియు
తెలియ గలరు చావు దెలియ లేరు,
చావు దెలియ లేని చదువుల' వే' లరా. వి. ౧౮౮

కొండంరాళ్లు ఁదెచ్చి, కోరిక ఁగట్టిన,
గుళ్ల లోన ఁదిరిగి కుళ్లనే' ల ?
పాయరాని శివుడు ప్రాణియై యుండంగ. వి. ౧౮౯

---

187. The recluseness of a dog! the meditations of a crane! the chanting of an ass! the bathing of a frog! ah, why will ye not try to know your own hearts!†

188. They read the entire (sastras) institutes, they transcribe them; these they can understand; but of death they know nothing! To what end is study that teaches us not how to die?

189. Why should you collect stones from the hill and build fine temples to walk about in them? Why torment yourselves so, while the God, as a living being, constantly dwells within you?

---

* Al. యాత్మ నెరుగుటకును యుడియాస జేయరో.

† Here the satirist reviles four of the ordained religious observances.

కులము వలనఁ గొంత, బలము వలనఁ గొంత,
కలిమి వలనఁ గొంత, గర్వమునను,
రంకు చదువుఁ జదివి రంకున బడుదురు. వి. ౧౯౦

విశ్వమును నడిపెడు విశ్వేశ్వరుండొకడు,
బ్రహ్మలకును నేల పాటి దక్కె ?
వనములోని కోతి వసుమతి నడుపునా వి. ౧౯౧

చదువు వానికన్న, చాకలి తా మేలు,
గురము *వేల్పుకన్న, కుక్క మేలు,
సర్వ సురలకన్న, సర్వేశ్వరుడు మేలు. వి. ౧౯౨

---

190. Through pride, arising partly from birth, partly from power, and partly from wealth, men follow licentious studies and fall into sin.

191. There is but one Lord of the universe who rules the world; is honour due to the rest of the Bramhas? † an ape of the woods might as well govern the earth.

192. Better is the *humble* washerman than the *empty* student; better is the house dog than the *inanimate* household goddess; and better than all demigods is the Lord of the universe.

---

* గురము, an *unauthorized* corruption of గృహము; which is, I believe, used by Vemana alone.

† The term "Brambas" would seem to be improperly used here for "gods." I have heard of but one temple to Bramha, and that was recently built by Vencatadri Naydu, at Chebol near Guntoor.

బూది పూఁతలెన్న, భుజముల పొంకాలు,
వ్రాలు లింగములును వరుస మతము,
లిక్కడఁ దగుఁ గాక, నక్కడఁ దగదెల్లు. వి. ౧౯౩

అడుగఁ దగు వారి నడిగిన,
నీడిన యెడఁగ, కొసర కొసరనీ లేనఁగా*
గడుసు-పడి, యాస చే, తా
న, డిగిన, దుర్మార్గ-వృత్తులగు రా, వేమా. ౧౯౪

అదనెఱిగిన మగువ, యనువెర్గు, చనువెర్గు;
ముదము తోడ మగని మోహమెరుగు,
విభుని శ్రేష్ఠ-గుణము వేశ్య తానెర్గునా? వి. †

---

193. All this smearing *your bodies* with *holy* ashes, these *sectarian* decorations on your shoulders, and *images* dangling from your necks, in short, your entire creeds, are of avail in this ‡ world alone, not in the next.

194. If you ask *aid* of one whom it is fit to solicit, and, on his granting it, if you redouble your importunity, and he say I can give no more; if then you be still obstinate *in solicitation* through cupidity, such conduct is utterly vile.

195. A woman who knows the right time for *this and that duty* is aware of what is proper and what is convenient; and with joy she recognizes the love of her lord. But how can a courtezan rightly value the virtues of a husband?

---

* ఈ - లేను, for ఇవ్వ - లేను.

† Al. సంతపాకలంజచనుమాన మెర్గునా.

‡ See note on II., 114. This is a satire on the lingam worshippers, a sect who are devoted to Siva.

ఆకటికి దోలంగు నాచార - విధులెల్ల !
చీకటికి దోలంగు చిత్త - శుద్ధి !
వేకటికి దోలంగు వెనకటి బిగువెల్ల. వి. ౧౯౬.

త్రాసును, పడిసే లంజయు
భాసుర గతినొక్కరూపు పరికింపంగా
వీసంబధికంబైనను,
వాసరమున నొక్కవంక వాలుర వేమా. ౧౯౭

నిరు పేదల రక్షించే
సరసుడు నెర దాత, గాక, సంపన్నుల దా
భరియించు - వాడు దాతయె ?
మెర - మెచ్చుల - దాత యతడు, మేదిని, వేమా.

తన్ను జూచి, యొరులు [దగ] మెచ్చ - వలెనని,
సొమ్ములెలమి బెట్టు, నెమ్మె మీర ;
నొరుల కొరకు దాన, యుబ్బుచు నుండును,
తన్ను దెలియ లేడు, ధరణి వేమ. ౧౯౯

196. He that is hungry forgets every religious tie, all purity of heart disappears in the dark,* and pregnancy destroys all former plumpness of body.

197. Why is a courtezan like a pair of scales? Because she balances daily in favor of those who will give her a penny more.†

198. He alone can be called beneficent who relieves the poor and miserable; but is he liberal who merely gives to the rich? He is liberal merely for the sake of applause.

199. He wears many ornaments and is puffed up with delight that others gaze at him. Surely he is unable to know himself!

* Or; all crimes seem excusable by night.

† This verse appears in manuscripts, but so greatly corrupted by ignorant transcribers, that the meaning was discovered only after comparing them all.

ధనము లేక యున్న, ధైర్యంబు నిలువదు ;
ధైర్యమొ' దవదే' ని, ధనము లేదు ;
ధనము ధైర్యమ' రయ, దగు భూమి - పతులకు. వి. *

ఇచ్చి పుచ్చు - కొన్న హితమైన మనువులు
తగ్గు - లేక, స' ల్లు, తామర వలె ;
కాచి, పూచి, పండి, కడు రమ్య మైయుండు. వి.

సతికి పతికి నైన, సంపద సంపదే ?
పుత్ర - సంపదలును భువిని మేలు,
సరిగ ముదిసి బ్రతుకు, సంపద సంపద. వి. ౨౦౨

---

200. If wealth leave us, resolution will not remain; and if spirit be wanting, wealth is nothing. Possessions and valor united constitute a king.

201. Marriage contracts, given and received with friendship, shall not lead to decrease, but shall flourish, *spreading* as a lotus plant *does over the* water, blossoming, budding, and bearing abundant fruit. †

202. Are riches the real wealth of either the wife or the husband? Surely the possession of a son is the first of blessings, and to grow old together is the greatest of all riches.

---

* A fourth line appears in some copies.
తగులుకొనుచునుండు ధరణి వేమ.

† I find a series of twelve verses regarding marriage in two copies of Vemana, but have retained this verse alone, the rest appearing spurious.

కడక నింద్రియములఁ గట్టి - వేయ - గ లేక,
చావు వచ్చున' పుడు, సన్యసించు
నాత్మ - జితము లేక, నందునా మోక్షము. వి.
అధిక సూక్ష్మమై'న యానందమె'రుగక,
మతియు లేక చదివి, మగ్నుడ' య్యె;
నతి - రహస్యమె' ల్ల నా జనుడె' రుగునా? వి.
కడకన' ఖిలమునకు నడి నాళమందు' న్న,
వేగు - చుక్క వంటె, వెలుగు, దిక్కు
వెల్గు కన్న దిక్కు వేరె' వ్వరు' న్నారు? వి. ౨౦౫
రామ - నామ - పఠనచే' మహి వాల్మీకి,
పరగ బోయ యయ్యు, బాపడ' య్యె;
కులము ఘనము గాదు, గుణము ఘనంబురా. వి.

---

203. During life he restrains not his lusts, but when death approaches he turns recluse: unless thou subdue thy heart, how shalt thou attain release.

204. Reading without understanding, or feeling that delight in wisdom which is the most refined of all, he is plunged *in ignorance*. How should this man know every recondite mystery.

205. That light, like the morning star that dwells in the inmost heart of every man, is our refuge. What asylum is there superior to this illumination? *

206. By *devoutly* repeating the *sacred* name of Rama Valmiki the savage † became a Bramin. Eminence depends not upon birth, but virtue.

---

* These expressions have reference to the mystic system.

† Boya or Nishada, nearly the same as the Erkela tribe. This is related of himself by the poet in the Ramayana. పఠన, *aliter* సూక్తి.

కలిమి గల్గనే' మి, కరుణ లేకు' ండెనా,
కలిమి యేల నిలుచు, కర్ములకును?
తేనె గూర్చి యీగ తెరువున బోవదా? ౨౦౭

చన్న - గవ రీతి, సంపద,
కొన్నాళ్ళకు వ్రేగుఁ జూపి, గొబ్బున వ్రాలుఁ,
వెన్నెల చీకటి సరి యగు
నన్నా శివ - లింగ - మాయల' న్నియు, వేమా? ౨౦౮

ఆలు పతి - సౌఖ్యములకి' [ల]
నా' లాయంబై' న దాని నాల' న వచ్చుఁ,
ఆలాగున గాకు' ండిన,
కాలుని పెను దూత గదర, కదియగ వేమా. ౨౦౯

తుమ్మ చెట్ల ముండ్లు తోడనె పుట్టును,
విత్తు లోననుం' డి వెడలిన' ట్లు,
మూర్ఖునకును బుద్ధి ముందుగా బుట్టునో. వి. ౨౧౦

---

207. If after acquiring wealth he use it not with liberality, how shall the sinner preserve it? Does not the bee, after storing up its honey, go its way, *and leave it to others?*

208. Riches flourish, like the charms of women, for a season, but rapidly fade away; as moonlight dies when a cloud passes over the sky.

209. If a woman be as a dwelling prepared for her husband's enjoyment, she is justly called a wife: and if not so, she is but the chief messenger of death.

210. As thorns are produced along with the mimosa tree, springing from the same seed, so does the evil mind of the stubborn fool grow up along with him.

"కామి గాని వాఁడు, కవి గాఁడు, రవి గాఁడు!"
కామి గాని, మోక్ష - కామి గాఁడు;
కామి యైన వాఁడు, కవి యగు, రవి యగు. వి.

కుక్క గోవు గాదు, కుందేలు పులి గాదు;
దోమ గజము గాదు, దొడ్డదైన
లోభి దాత గాఁడు, లోకంబు లోపల. వి. ౨౧౨

కూడు గుడిచి లెస్స కూర్చున్న వాఁడైన *
నాఁడు దానిఁ గన్న నట్టె తగులు,
నన్న రసము, యొడలికతి మదంబగు సుమీ. వి.

---

211. "What poet or what god is there free from the darts of love?" this is mere desire, not love of wisdom. Poets and demigods are all mere libertines. †

212. What comparison in the world is there between a dog and a cow, a hare and a tiger, or a gnat and an elephant, be it as large as it may; or between a miser and, a liberal man?

213. When a man has feasted and sits at his case should he see a woman, he is touched with love; the vigour given by food fills the body with cupidity.

---

* Al. మనుజుండు, and జనుఁడుతాఁ.

† Here, as in some other verses, I have given rather a paraphrase than a close translation, which would not convey the idea intended. The word *Ravi* appears to be a mere echo to *Cavi*. The first line probably is a quotation.

దేవ - పూజ సేయ, దివ్య - భోగము గల్గు,
తత్వమె' ఱిగనే' ని, దైవ - సముడే,
యేమి లేని నరునకే' గతి లేదు ర. వి. ౨౧౪

రెండవ యాశ్వాసము సంపూర్ణము.

---

214. Through the performing of divine worship is divine enjoyment attained. He who knows the truth is verily * as a god. But he who has nothing, shall attain to nothing.

* This intensive is implied by the syllable *e* added to samudu. See Matth, xiii., 12.

END OF BOOK II.

వేమన పద్యములు.

మూడవ ఆశ్వాసము.

కలియుగముననున్న కాపుకులానకు
వేమన దన కీర్తి విక్రయించె;
నున్న ధర్మమెల్ల నుర్విలో నరులకు,
కోరఁ బెట్టి, పరముఁ గోరి, వేమ. ౧

చెవినిల్లుగట్టి చెప్పెను వేమన,
బట్టబయలునందు బ్రహ్మమనుచు
బుద్ధిఁగలిగి యందుఁ బొంది సుఖించుఁడీ. * వి. ౨

BOOK III.

1. In this iron age † has Vemana, by his celebrity rendered the farmer tribe honorable; striving to attain to the Supreme Good, he has dealt forth to all men every truth he knew.

2. Incessantly ‡ did Vemana speak in our ears, saying "Evident and manifest is the deity; be wise, attain it, and be for ever happy!"

* In some copies a fourth line is added.
సుకవులైన వారు సుస్థిరముగ.

† The four ages (Yuga) of the world, denominated Crita, Treta, Dwapara, and Cali, answer to the Golden, Silver, Brazen, and Iron ages spoken of in the poets of Europe.

‡ Literally: Making his dwelling at our ear. This colloquial phrase occurs also in the *Mrityanjaya Vilasa*, where Rati Devi (Psyche) exclaims, on the death of her husband Cupid,
సీ. చెవినిల్లు గట్టుక చెప్పిన నామాట
అవునాని వినవైతి, యయ్యొ మదన!

పొంకముగను మనసు పోనీక సర్వేశు
వంక - నిల్పు వాడు, వంశ వరుడు,
వంక నిల్పకు' న్న వచ్చునా పదవులు ? వి. ౩

ఉండి యుండి జ్ఞాని యుగములు చని పోవ
ప్రాణ హాని లేదు ప్రళయమునను
ప్రాణ - హాని యైన పరమా' త్ము గలసునో? వి. ౪

గురువు తాన యినను, హరుని ఁదా ఁజూపును,
బ్రహ్మ - లోకమ' తడు పార ఁజూపు,
శిష్యున' రసి పట్టి చీకటి ఁబాపురా? వి. ౫

---

3. He who duly restrains his heart, and directs it to the Lord of all, is the noblest of his tribe; unless he so direct it, how can he attain to happiness? *

4. He that has wisdom shall live for ever; even in the final destruction his soul shall not perish: at the time of that destruction he shall be united to the Great Spirit.

5. He who is a teacher will instruct others regarding God; † he will plainly reveal the celestial abode; he looks well to his pupil, and dissipates the darkness of his ignorance.

---

* *Padavi* is here a Telugu word, and distinct from the similar Sanskrit word.

† See on II., 67.

ధనమే మూలము జగతికి,
ధనమే మూలంబు సకల ధర్మంబులకున్ ;
గొనమే * మూలము సిరులకు,
మనమే మూలంబు ముక్తి- మహిమకు వేమా. ౬

కడగి గాలి లేని గగనంబు భంగిని,
బలు తరగలు లేని జలధి మాడ్కి,
నిర్వికారమునను నిశ్చలత్వమున తా
ను' ండెనేని, ముక్తి యొనరు వేమ. ౭

నీళ్లు పోసి కడిగి, నిత్యంబు శోధించి,
కూడు బెట్టి, మీద కోక గట్టి
యేమి పాట్లు బడుదురీ' దేహమునకి' ల? వి. ౮

---

6. In this world riches form the chief objects; on wealth does the due performance of every duty depend; virtue is the origin of every blessing; and final beatitude depends on *the conduct* of our own hearts.

7. If thy heart become calm as the breezeless firmament and the unruffled waveless deep, changeless and unfluctuating—this is denominated freedom!

8. We continually pour water over our bodies, and wash, feed? and dress them; how many cares we suffer for the perishable body!

---

* This line generally stands thus:

గుణమే మూలము స్త్రీలకు.

But to preserve the prasa rhyme గొనం (the tadbhava of గుణం) substituted; as also (సిరి *i.e.* శ్రీ) for స్త్రీ a conjectural emendation, which I think the sense requires.

గద్దె, గణము, నిద్ర - కలలు, కోరి కెలుస్న,
ముదమొ' సంగు శకునములును ఁజెలగు,
ప్రశ్నలు పది వేలు, పరికించి చూడంగ'
నవును కాకపోవున [వని] వేమ.

లేడు లేడ నినను లేడు లేనే లేడు,
కాడు కాడ' టన్న, కానె కాడు ;
తోడు తోడ' నినను, తోడనే తోడౌను. వి. ౧౦

శివుని మీద మనసు స్థిరముగాను' ంచిన,
నౌ' ను మోక్షమ' రయునౌ' నదౌ' ను,
శివుని మీద మనసు చీమంత తప్పిన,
కాదు, కాదు, ముక్తి కాదు, వేమ. ౧౧

---

9. Fortune-telling, possession *by a demon*, dreams of sleep, idle wishes, and pleasing auguries, with divinations of all sorts, * turn out true or false, *as it may happen: who can rely on them?*

10. If thou say *of the divinity* that he exists not, he is no more accessible; if thou say he is not, then *with regard to thee* he is of no avail; if thou call him thy helper, he will surely aid thee.†

11. If thou stay thy mind firmly on the deity, beatitude shall be thine, shall be thine! if thy heart swerve even in the least ‡ from him, never shall heaven be thy lot.

---

* Padi vela. See on II,. 42 and 82.

† A verse the sense of which is obscure: it is hardly translateable; the second line may be rendered differently: this negative when placed absolutely signifying " it is naught or of no avail." Thus *cani-vadu* is an enemy. The next verse contains similar expressions.

‡ Lit, as much as an ant's length.

తల్లికెదురు కొనుట, తండ్రికెదురు కొంట, *
యన్నకెదురు కొనుట, యరయ మూఁడు,
పాతకములనెరిగి వర్తింపగా వలె. వి. ౧౨

లోభ, మోహములను, ప్రాభవములు దప్పు,
తలచిన పనులెల్లఁ దప్పి చనును;
తామొకటి దలచిన, దైవమొక్కటి దల్చు. వి.

వరలు రత్న-సమితి, వలెఁ గూర్చు ధాన్యంబు.
జక్కఁ దంచి, వండి మిక్కుటముగ,
సుష్ఠు భోజనములుఁ జూరగానిడు వాఁడు
చెప్పనేల? వాఁడె శివుడు వేమ. ౧౪

ఒకటి క్రిందనొక్కటొనర లబ్ధముఁ బెట్టి,
వలనుగ గుణియింప వరుస బెరుగు,
నట్టి రీతినుండునౌదార్య-ఫలములు. వి. ౧౫

---

12. Conduct thyself so as to beware of three sins—disobedience to thy mother, rebellion against thy father, and despising thy elder brother.

13. Avarice and lust are sufficient to ruin any dominion; all that we have devised shall fail and perish; the thoughts of men are one way, and the providence of God is another.

14. He who collects grain, precious as gems *in a famine* dresses it, and liberally distributes that excellent food, is no less than a beneficent deity.

15. As surely as figures added to figures form a total, so surely shall liberality and beneficence lead to wealth.

---

* This is an inelegant form of the verbs.

అన్నమ' రుగన' తనిక' న్నంబు ఁబెట్టిన,
పార వేసు, దాని ఫలిత మే' మి ?
ధనికునకు నొ' సంగు దానముల' టువలె. వి. ౧౬

ఇరుగు పొరుగు వారి కై' నయు సంపద ఁజూచి,
తమకు లేద' టన్న, ధర్మ మే' మి ? *
ధర్మ మ' న్న తొల్లి దన్నుక చచ్చిరి,
కర్మ ఫలము నేడు ఁగలిగె' వేమ. ౧౭

ఆకల' న్న వారిక' న్నంబు బెట్టితె,
హారునక' ర్పితముగనా' రగించు,
ధన - విహీనునకి' డు దానముల' టువలె. వి. ౧౮

---

16. He whose digestion is weak throws away food as unprofitable; and equally useless are presents made to the rich.

17. Why should a man grieve because he lacks the wealth which he sees heaped up in the houses of others? In his former birth he died without attempting to perform any charitable act, and now reaps the fruit of that life.

18. To give food to the hungry is as meritorious as offering it in sacrifice; so great is the charity of relieving the poor.

---

* Al. తనకులాడు or తిన్నను' ఁద్రు for ధర్మ మే' మి. This verse would seem spurious.

కలిగి పెట్ట లేని కర్మ - జీవులకెల్ల,
తిరిపెమును దొరకదు దీనులార !
తెలియఁ జూచు కొనుడు దృష్టాంతమి' ది మీకు. వి.

తిరిపెగాఁడ' యినను తిరిపెమొ' త్తినయట్టి
తిరిపెమ'ందు తాను తిరిపెమి' డిన,
తిరిపెము తిరిపెమున' దిగబడిపోవురా. వి. ౨౦

తాము బలిమిఁ బెట్ట తమకు తామే కల్గు,
నడుగని' డిన తామున' డుగ గలుగు,
ని' ందునీ' ని వానికె' ందును గల్గదు. వి. ౨౧

---

19. Those who have and bestow not (O ye poor!) shall in their next birth not receive even alms. Know and understand this; it is evident to all men; say not that you are deluded.*

20. If a mendicant bestows as alms any part of what he has received in charity, this renders his begging *not disgraceful, but* honourable.

21. The alms that are bestowed without being asked shall, unsought, return to you; whatever we give, being asked, so much shall return on our asking: and he who bestows nothing shall receive nothing.

---

* Here and in some other passages the doctrine of transmigration is inculcated very strongly. We may, however, doubt whether these verses were written by Vemana, who has elsewhere pointed out the absurdity of this belief.

తాము గడన సేయు ధనము తమది యని,
నమ్మి యుండ్రు వెఱ్ఱి నరులు, భువిని,
తామునొకరికిచ్చు, ధనమింతియే కాక,
కడమది తమకేల గలుగు వేమ. ౨౨

తాముఁ దినకన' టుల ధర్మము సేయక,
కొడుకులక' ని ధనముఁ గూడ బెట్టి,
తెలియఁ జెప్ప లేక తీరిపోయిన వెన్క,
సొమ్ము పరులన'ంటు, జూడు వేమ. ౨౩

దాచిన ధనమునకు, తానును కొడుకును
వాంఛ బడుటె కాని, వట్టి భ్రమలు ;
భాగ్య - హీనునకును, ఫలము లభించునా ? వి. ౨౪

---

22. If you consider your possessions as your own, fools alone will agree with you. That alone is yours which you have bestowed on others, the rest is not at your disposal.*

23. If thou consume it not thyself, nor bestow it in charity, but hoard up thy wealth for thy sons, and then die without pointing out *where it is buried*, all thy riches shall fall to the lot of strangers!

24. If you have buried your wealth what good can you, or your son derive from it? you merely suffer anxiety regarding it. A luckless wretch can never have any real enjoyment.

---

* See II., 75.

భాగ్యహీనునకును, పరుసవేది దొరుక
నదియు నిల్వద పుడు వదలు గాక ;
వానతోడ వచ్చు వడగండ్లు నిల్చునా? వి. ౨౫

ధన - విహీనుడైన తండ్రి గర్భంబున,
భాగ్య - పురుషుడొ కడు [పరగ] బుట్టి,
బహుళ ధనము గలిగి భద్ర - మార్గంబున,
పరులకు పకరించి, ప్రబలు వేమ. ౨౬

ఇహమునందు బాధలెన్నైన బడ వచ్చు
యముని బాధ - లేకనే మర వలెను,
పరుల - బాధ లేక బ్రతుకుడీ, నరులార. వి. ౨౭

*వల్ల వైపు లేక, వాగ్దత్తము టుచేసి,
యదిగో యిదిగో యనుచు నాశ పెట్టి
గడువు పెట్టి రేపు గడియగా నిమ్మని
గడియ లోన బడియె, గదర వేమ. ౨౮

25. If an unlucky fool should even find the philosopher's stone, it would never remain in his hands, but vanish : it would melt away like the hailstones that come with rain.

26. If one whose destiny is good be born even of a luckless father, he will attain to wealth, and by heedfully benefiting others, shall become mighty.

27. Whatever pain we may suffer in this life, let us be careful to escape from the pains of hell ; injure not others, O men, and live for ever !

28. He who, without considering his own means, makes oral promises and deludes you, saying Here *it is*, or There, *take it*,* and, after fixing a period for payment, says I will pay you to-morrow, he shall suddenly perish.

* The words *idugo* and *adugo* appear to belong to the class grammatically termed *Cala* In some manuscipts the verse begins with the words వెల్లనా కెరుగక which give no clear sense.

పరులకు' పకరింప, పాప - క్షయంబ' గు
పరులకు' పకరింప, పట్టు కొమ్మ,
పరులకు' పకరింప పరలోక - సాధన ; ౨౯
పరులకు' పకరింప, బలిమి వేమ.

అర్థవంతు - సొమ్మునా' సింతుర, ర్థుల ;
వ్యర్థికీని సొమ్ము వ్యర్థమౌ ను
వ్యర్థమై' న సొమ్ము వ్యర్థుల 'జేరురా. వి. ౩౦

ధర్మ - కంటకుండు ధనముచే గర్వించి,
సకల సంపదలను చాల బొరలి,
కడకు, తాను మేలు గానక, చెడి పోవు. వి. ౩౧

ఇంతి తనదు పేరునె' ల్ల కాలంబును,
ప్రజలు దలచున' ట్లు ప్రతిభ గాంచె,
నె' ంతికి పతి - భక్తి యెంతె' న వచ్చును ? వి. ౩౨

---

29. Beneficence to others shall cover thy sins ; it shall be a stay to thee ; it is a means of attaining the world above ; it forms a refuge for thee.

30 The beggar naturally seeks for the substance of the wealthy ; and that which is bestowed on no mendicant shall perish : and those who are ready to perish shall enjoy that perishing wealth.

31. He who values himself on his wealth and bestows none on others, revelling in riches, shall, in the end, perish and never see good.

32. When a woman has *by her virtues* acquired lasting celebrity, and men remember her excellence—how can we oo highly esteem her devotion to her husband ?

ధర్మమునకు కీడుఁ దలచిన వాడు, తా
దుష్ట - మార్గుడై గును, దోవ చెడును ;
గురువు పత్నిగవయ ఁగోరెడు - వాడు, తా
మొదలు, సెడును, ఁజూడ మొనసి వేమ. 33

అలయ చేసి మలచి యాడిగెండ్లు మలిగెండ్లు, *
తిరిపెమి డెదు, కటిక దేబలెల్ల,
నెలమి మన్ను దినెడు నెర్ర లౌదురు సుమీ. వి.

మత్సరంబు, మదము, మమకారమ నియెడి
వ్యసనములను దగిలి నుసల బోక,
పరులకు పకరించి, పరము నమ్మికను, ండి,
యొనరుచుండు, రాజ - యోగి. వేమ. 35

---

33. He who meditates opposition to virtuous acts, becomes an evil doer, and shall perish from the way : and he who thinks upon the spouse of his preceptor, shall utterly perish.

34. Those utterly worthless wretches who, when they winnow grain, give away the dregs and scum * as charity —shall *in their next transmigration* be born earthworms.

35. He who has ceased from envy, lust, and selfishness, who is not agitated by influence of any passion, who is benevolent to others and remains in the faith to the Great Spirit—he is the perfect man.

---

* The chaff at the top and the dirt at the bottom of the sieve. Al. అలిగెలు మలిగెలు, *i, e.* tares and pebbles.

దాన - ధర్మములును, దయయు, సత్యము' నీతి,
వినయ, ధైర్య, ధుర్య, వితరణములు
రాజు - పాలిటికి' వి రాజ - యోగంబులు. వి. ౩౬

క్రొవ్వు బట్టు, పొరలు క్రూర కర్మల పొరల్,
నవ్వు జేసిన' ట్టి రవ్వ పొరల '
ఎ' వ్వరైననే' మి, యినజు వాకిటగాని,
యవ్వలికిని బోవున' టర, వేమ! ౩౭

---

36. Donation, alms, kindness, truth, wisdom, humility, valor, resolution, liberality : these *virtues*, if they fall to the share of a prince, constitute the quality denominated royal.*

37. He becomes fat, and wallows in the frauds of his evil disposition, and empty slander of others : when a man arrives at the gate of hell, be he who he may, he will suffer the retribution of this.†

---

* Terms belonging to any peculiar creed or system of philosophy usually convey a sense different from that which a literal translation requires. In this verse and some others I have therefore used a slight latitude of explanation, leaving the reader to collect the precise import of the technical words in question from a comparison of various passages.

† The word *pora* is in this verse used in several senses: such double meanings (in rhetoric denominated *slesha*) are used in all the modern Telugu poets.

రోగిన' రసిన'ట్టి లోకోప - కారులు.
భోగ - భాగ్యములను, బొంది, తుదను,
పూర్వ - వాసన జెగి, పురహరు తావున,
మ్రొగుచు' ందుర' ట్టి, మొనసి. వేమా. ౩౮

జ్ఞానమె' న్న గురువు ; జ్ఞాన హీనము బుద్ధి ;
రెంటి సందు రిమ్మ రేచు నపుడు ;
రిమ్మ దెలిసెనే' ని రెండో' క రూపురా. * వి. ౩౯

పుట్టిన' దియు మొదలు, పురుషుడే' కాలంబు,
పాపమె, రగి, శుద్ధ పశువుగాక,
ముదిసి యోగి కరణి, ముద మొ' ప్పగావలె. వి. ౪౦

---

38. Those benefactors of mankind who regard the sick patient shall attain all enjoyment and wealth: these shall not be affected by the sins of their former births, shall live before God, resounding † *his praise*.

39. Wisdom is the teacher: the *human* heart is *absolute* ignorance; but when we fall into giddy state of fluctuation between these two *principles*—until *that giddiness* is dissipated, neither of these can be distinguished.

40. From his birth upwards let a man constantly beware of sin; let him not become degraded to a brute; but grow old in holiness and attain to bliss.

---

* రెండో'క రూపురా substituted for రెండుండి సోపురా which, though appearing in three manuscripts, gives no clear sense.

† This verb *mogu* certainly is generally applied (as in verse 30, Book I.) to nanimate objects; but is also *colloquially* used, as it is in this passage.

సకలాకారుడనంతుడు
సకలాత్మలయందు సర్వ-సాక్షియుదానై,
సకలమున నిర్వికారుం
డకలంక-స్థితిని, బ్రహ్మమన బడు, వేమా. ౪౧

నేనెవ్వడనని తలచడు,
మానసమున పుడమి లోని మనుజుండకటా!
కానడు తను సకలంబును,
మానుగ గనుగొనుట యెట్లు, మహిలో. వేమా? ౪౨

జనుడు తెలివినొంద, చంచలింపదు మది,
దైవమును దెలిసిన తగులు బుద్ధి,
[త్రిపుర] భాను-జూచి తిమిరంబు నిలుచునా? వి.

---

41. He whose form is universal, who is eternal, who himself witnesses all that passes in every heart, who exists immutably throughout the universe, and is free from all shadow *of darkness—this being* is called God.

42. No man in the world considers truly who he is; alas, he cannot know his whole nature! how shall man learn to know himself.

43. If a man attain wisdom, his heart will not alter; if he know the deity, wisdom shall be joined to him: when the sun is seen how shall darkness remain?

పగలు రేయు మరచి, భావంబును మరచి,
తాను నేన, నయెడి తలపు మరచి,
యుండు వాని నె' ంచను' త్తము యోగి, రా. వి. ౪౪
మంట, లోహమందు, మాకుల, శిలలందు,
పటము, గోడల' ందు, ప్రతిమల' ందు,
తన్ను దెలుసుకొరకు తగలదా పరమా' త్మ ? వి.
మనసు లోని వాని, మానుగా దెలిసిన,
ను' ర్వి - జనులు వాని యోగి యండ్రు ;
నీవు నిన్నె' రుంగ, నీవె, పో, శివుడవు. వి. ౪౫
మాట లోని వాని, మహిమ తా దెలియక,
మాటఁ దెలియ లేక, మమతఁ జిక్కి,
మాటఁ దెలిసెనే' ని, మరి యాత్మ యోగి రా. వి.

44. The man that has attained perfection draws no distinctions between day and night, the mind and universal nature, or himself and another man.*

45. Neither in earth nor metal, wood or stone, painted walls, or images, does that Great Spirit reside so as to be perceived.

46. He *alone* among the sons of men merits the title of "saint" (yogi †) who knows the deity that dwells in his heart; know thyself, and thou shalt become the deity.

47. Ignorant of the greatness of Him who dwells in a word,‡ and heedless of our words, we are snared in our lusts. He who can truly comprehend this word is the real saint.

---

* Losing all individuality, by becoming resolved into the universe is a leading doctrine in the Vedanta creed.

† *Yogi*, generally translated *hermit*, or *recluse*, being derived from *yuga*, union, implies one who is *united* to the deity, by the particular act of meditation denominated *yogam*.

‡These and similar mystic expressions appertain to the Vedanta system of theology; from their obscurity they admit of several interpretations.

వ్రేయ వ్రేయ - గాను, విత్తనమ నిపించు,
వ్రేయ వ్రేయ, ప్రబల వృక్షమ గును,
తెలియ తెలియ, వాడు దేవుడ’ నందగు. వి. ౪౮

గడనగల పురుషు గనుగొని,
యడుగులకును మడుగులి’ డుదుర’ తివెలు ధరలో,
గడన విడు, పురుషు గనుగొని,
నడ పీనుగ వచ్చెన’ ందు, నాతులు వేమా. ౪౯

వంటు దప్పిన’ పుడు వంటకము విషంబు,
కంట జూడగానె, కంటగించు,
కంటకమున దిన్న, కడి గండమై వచ్చు. వి. ౫౦

వంటి వచ్చిన’ పుడు, వంటకమ’ మృతంబు,
కంటికి’ ంపుగాను, కానుపించు,
నొ’ డల తినిన తిండి, వడి మించగను దోరు. వి. ౫౧

48. That which is cast and sown is called seed; by being sown it becomes a tree; and by the gradual acquisition of wisdom, a man becomes *part of* the deity.

49. If they see a man of property, women will lay their very vests for his feet to walk on; but if they meet one who has lost his possessions, they hold him no better than a walking corpse.

50. *If eaten* out of due time even food turns to poison; if we even see it with the eye we loath it; whatever you eat with disgust is fatal *as venom*.

51. In its due season food is *refreshing as* ambrosia, and appears agreeable to the eye; but if it disagrees with us, it is poison.

కలిగి ధర్మమి' వ్వఁ గానని వారును,
గలిగి తినఁజాల, గ్రాఁగు వారు,
కలిమిఁనె చట జూడఁ, గానక చెడుదురు. వి. ౫౨

అల్లువాని మృతికినా' త్మ జింతించును?
తనయు మృతికి, దానె దల్లడిల్లు;
పుణ్య పురుషు మృతికి, భూమిలో జనులకీ,
యుగము గ్రుంగిన ట్టులు,' ండు వేమ. ౫౩

సకల విద్య నేర్చి చచ్చి, బ్రతుకు విద్య,
యొ కటి నేరమ' నుచును ర్వ జనులు,
కటకట బడుదురు, కడ హాని దెలియరు. వి. ౫౪

---

52. Those who will bestow nothing in charity, who consume not their riches but pine for more, shall perish without enjoying any comfort.

53. At the death of his son-in-law a man grieves in soul; at his son's death he is plunged in sorrow; but when a good man dies the whole world grieves as though on the point of perishing.

54. After learning all other branches of wisdom men remain ignorant that they are to die and be reproduced: alas they perish without knowing any thing of *impending* destruction.

దూర - దృష్టి ఁగనరు, దుడ్డిన * దనుకను,
జారు పట్టె రుగరు, పడిన దనుక ;
దండ - సాధ్యుల,' రయ, ధర్మ - సాధ్యులు గారు,
భూమి జనులు; వెర్రి బుద్ధి, వేమ. ౫౫

ముష్టి, వేప చెట్టు, మొదలుగా ప్రజలకు,
పరగ మూలికలకు పనికి వచ్చు,
నిర్దయాత్మకుండు నీచుడై ందునకును,
పనికి రాడు గదర పరగ వేమ. ౫౬

ప్రభువు కోతియైన, ప్రగడలు పందులు!
సైనికుండు' పక్కి, సేన పసులు ;
ఏన్గుల శ్వచయములె' లుకలు, పిల్లులు. వి. ౫౭

---

55. They possess no foresight before evil actually touches them; until they fall, they know not that they are slipping; these are subjects for punishment, not for mercy: how unwise are all the men of the earth!

56. Even the poison-nut, the *bitter* margosa, and the rest are useful as drugs; but the unfeeling vile wretch is utterly unprofitable.

57. Where the king is an ape, his ministers are mere swine; where the general is a chicken, his troops are mere cattle; his elephants and horses are no better than mice and cats set in array.

---

* Al. దొడ్డిన and తొట్టిన. The word given in the text is peculiar to the western districts.

తిట్టినే ని, మొట్టు; మొట్టితే, కొట్టును;
కొట్టినే ని, యముడు కొద్ది పరుచు;
కోపమొంచ, చెడ్డ పాపము, నర - హత్య. వి. ౫౮

కోపమునను ఘనత, కొంచెమై పోవును,
కోపమునను మిగుల గోడు (జెందు,
కోపము డచెనే ని, కోరికెల్లి, డేరు. వి. ౫౯

కోపమునను, నరక - కూపము (జెందును;
కోపమునను గుణము కొంచెము గును;
కోపమునను బ్రతుకు కొంచెమై పోవును. వి. ౬౦

రాజు మాట వలెను రసికుడా డగ వలె;
నెంత పనికిను బికి, యెగర రాదు;
కదిసి యెగిరెనే ని, గ్రహ - సమానము గాదె,
దొడ్డు, కొంచెమే, ల దొరుకు, వేమ? వి. ౬౧

---

58. If you abuse a man he will cuff you; if you thump him, he will thrash you; and next follow murder;* anger is the greatest of sins, it leads to manslaying.

59. Through anger we suffer degradation; wrath leads to grief; repress anger, and all thy wishes shall be attained.

60. By means of anger does hell become our lot through anger is every good quality diminished; by anger is life shortened.

61. A man of delicacy will speak in conformity to what the king says; on no occasion will he be puffed up *with pride*: should he exalt himself, he is *pernicious* as a demon, and shall gain nothing, either more or less.

---

* Lit. If he strikes, Pluto will take possession. In the end of the lats lines *Dwija-hatya* sometimes occur.

సాధు - సజ్జనులను సంతరించిన వాడు,
ప్రజల సంతసంబు పరచు వాడు,
కదసి, శాత్రవులను కరుణ జూచిన వాడు,
పాదుకొన్న ముక్తి - పరుడు వేమ. ౬౨

[పరగ] లేమి చేత, బంధువుల్ పగవారు;
పరగ లేమి చేత, పరము దప్పు;
పరగ లేమి చేత, పరపతి దప్పురా. వి. ౬౩

నేర్చి' నడతున' న్న, నేరమి [తా] వచ్చు;
నోర్చి నడతున, న్న, నో' ర్ప రాదు;
కూర్చి నడతున' న్న కూడంగని' య్యదు. వి. ౬౪

ధనము లేమి యనెడు దావానలంబును,
తన్ను జెరుచును, దరి దాపు జెరుచు,
ధనము లేమి చూడ, దలచనే' పాపంబు. వి. ౬౫

---

62. He who retains men of prudence and virtue in his service, and acts so as to gain the goodwill of men, and is beneficent *even* to his enemies, is the well-grounded aspirant after beatitude.

63. Poverty makes a man's relations his foes; by poverty we fail of attaining heaven; and through want we lose credit with the lender.

64. If you say "I know how to conduct myself," this will lead to ignorance: If you say "I am humble," this is no humility. If you say "I can manage the matter," you will, *through pride*, fail of it.

65. When a man falls into the fierce flame of poverty he himself perishes and ruins every one near him; poverty indeed is looked upon as *absolutely* a sin!

కాపు బలిమి యున్న, కరణానక' ది బల్మి ;
కరణము బలిమెల్ల, కాపు బలిమి ;
కాపు సంతసంబు కరణము సంతోష -
మ' రసి చూడ, లోకమ' ందు, వేమ. ౬౬

కనక గ్రామమునకు కారణ - కర్తలి'
ద్దు' ండ నగుచును' భయులు' ండిరే' ని,
గండ - పక్షి - యుగళము' ండిన కీతిని,
యుద్ది గూడి, బ్రతుకుచు' ండ్రు, వేమ. ౬౭

చేకొనుచును తమకు చెయి సాగిన' ంతలో,
చెడిన ప్రజల రక్ష సేయ లేని,
తనదు సాగు' టే' మి తన, తనువ' ది యేమి? వి. ౬౮

---

66. The strength of the farmer constitutes the power of the Carnam ;* and the might of the Carnam increases that of the farmer : all that the Carnam enjoys originates in the farmer.

67. So these two men are the doers of all that is effected in the village : if both of them continue watchful, they are powerful as a two headed eagle ; † inseparable, they shall prosper.

68. When a man has attained *power* and dominion, if he does not succour the poor and ruined, of what profit is his influence or his existence ?

---

* This term nearly answers to our old word *reeve*, or *head borough*. He is the village accountant.

† A griffin, or roc : creatures alluded to in the Arabian Nights.

దోపుని' చ్చు వాడు, తోడనే నెర దాత,
దోచుకున్న - వాడు, ద్రోహి యయ్యె;
ప్రాపుఁ జూపు వాడు, పరమ - పుణ్యుండ' య్యె,
ప్రాపుఁ జెరుచు * వాడు, పశువు వేమ. ౬౯

కాలము తనకి' క చాలా
కాలము గలద' ంచును' న్న, కాలమునందుఁ,
కూళుఁడు, తనుఁ దాఁ దెలియక,
కూలెను తొలి - బాముని' ందు; గొబ్బున, వేమా. ౭౦

కూట - వాసి యగుచు, గుణములఁ బచరించి,
నీట నీడ వలెను, నిలిచి యుండు,
ను' దక - ఘటము బగులను' పరిఁ జూచిన గాని,
సూర్యుడో' కడు గాడు, చూడు, వేమ. ౭౧

---

69. He who allows himself to be plundered is at once called a great benefactor ; but those that plunder him are offenders ; he who protects others is the best of men ; but he who forfeits his aid is no better than a brute.

70. He who imagines he has yet a long life before him, the fool who, while living, knows not himself, when he perishes shall suddenly feel *the punishments* incurred in his previous transmigrations.

71. He who becomes converted into the first of all beings, who duly weighs *the characteristic* properties, and receives light *from the deity* like the reflection of the sun in water, after *this mortals* vessel breaks, shall be re-united to the universal deity.

---

* Al. ఁజెడిన.

ప్రాఁతఁ జేసిన వర్తనల్ వదట* ఁగలిపి,
క్రొత్త వర్తన జేతురు, కోడెకాండ్రు;
కన్న *తల్లిని విడనా' డి కష్ట పెట్టి,
యన్య కాంతల పోషించు' నట్లు, వేమ. ౭౨

వాసి, వర్తనలును, వరుసను మర్యాద,
దప్పి, నడిచెనే' ని తగులు కీడు;
వదలద' ప్పుడు దాఁకున' ది తప్పితే, తుది
ముసలి ముప్పునై' న మునుఁగు, వేమ. ౭౩

ఇంగలంబు తోడని' లనె' ల్పు తోడను,
పరుని యాలితోడ, పతితు తోడ,
సరసమా' డుటె' ల్ల, చావుకు మూలంబు. వి. ౭౪

---

72. Young men trample on the conduct they formerly practised, and adopt new manners. They bid their mother begone, they afflict her, and give their wealth to strange women.

73. If he depart from the rules of kith and kin, of rule and custom, he shall suffer misery, it shall not depart from him; and should he at first elude it, it will befall him in decrepit old age.

74. To sport with fire, or with a light man, with your neighbour's wife, or with a fallen wretch—all tends to death.

---

* From.

† This is the *Tetagiti* metre. The translation is paraphrastic. The creed here inculcated teaches that, as every vessel contains a portion of the universe, which, after a temporary separation, is re-united to the great whole, so spirits, when released from the body, are again mingled with the deity.

మనసు నిల్పినట్టి మర్మజ్ఞులగు వారు,
గరిమ మోక్షపదముఁ గన్న వారు;
చెట్టుఁ బెట్టు, ఫలము చేకొనడా తాను? వి. ౭౫

తను దాఁ దెలుసుట, తత్వము,
తనకన్యులు బోధసేయ, ధరలో గలరే?
తను దాఁ దెలియకనుండిన,
తనకే వరుఁ దెలుప లేరు, తథ్యము, వేమా. ౭౬

మంచి వారు లేరు, మహి మీద వెదకిన,
కష్టులెందరైన గలరు భువిని
పసిడి లేదు గాని, పదడెంత లేదయా! వి. ౭౭

మాటలాడ నేర్చి, మనసు గరుగఁజేసి,
పరగ ప్రియము పుట్ట, పలుకకున్న,
నొకరి చేతి సొమ్ములూరక వచ్చునా? వి. ౭౮

---

75. Those who restrain their hearts, and know the great secret, shall effectually behold the abode of bliss; shall not he who plants a tree, reap its fruit.

76. To know one's self is the chief object; * is there any other who can explain this to us? If we know not ourselves, none can teach us.

77. The good are rarely found; the wicked are as numerous as you will; as gold is more rare than dust.

78. If you learn to speak acceptably, and to melt the heart *of your protector*, and addreshim so as to gain his goodwill, *you will succeed*; but will empty words obtain you any good?

* Tatvam.

అండములనుఁ బుట్టున' [లర] ప్రాణులు కొన్ని,
బుద్బుదములఁ బుట్టు, పురుగులె' ల్ల,
స్వేదమునను బుట్టు, జీవులు కొన్ని రా. వి. ౭౯

అన్నమ' ధికమై' నన' దియుఁ దాఁ జంపునా,
యన్నమ' ంటకున్న, నా' త్మనొచ్చు,
చంపనో' ంప బువ్వ చాలదా? వెయ్యే' ల? * వి. ౮౦

ఆశలు' డుగ గాని, పాశ - ముక్తుడు గాడు,
ముక్తుడై' న గాని, మునియు గాడు;
మునియునై' తె గాని, మోహంబులు' డుగవు. వి.

చంప దలచు రాజు చనువ' గ్గలంబి' చ్చు;
చెరపను' న్న పగర చెలిమి సేయు;
కరువను' న్న పాము సెరి దాచుకొని యుండు. వి.

---

79. Some animals are born from eggs; all reptiles are produced from spawn;† and some living beings originate in sweat.

80. Food in excess causes death, and too great abstinence endangers life; food, then, is the origin of life and death.

81. Till his lusts are quelled, no man can be freed from earthly ties: until he is thus freed he is no hermit;‡ unless thou become an ascetic, thy lusts shall not be destroyed.

82. The king that wishes to slay you will cherish you liberally; he shows kindness to those enemies he hopes to destroy: like a snake that lies in wait will he conceal *his designs*.

---

* *Vey ela*; literally "Why *use* a thousand *arguments*?" † This word the lexicons interpret as "a bubble," but a different sense is here requisite.
‡ *Muni*, a hermit or ascetic: more literally, a monk or recluse (Gr. *monachus*, one who lives alone). The root of the word *muni* is obscure but the derivative "maunam, silence, taciturnity," gives the idea.

చెరుకు లోననైన చెడ్డ గుణంబున్న
తీసి వేయకున్న తినగ బొసగ -
దంతిపురము ద్రోహి యాంతఁజెట్లుండు, రా. వి.
తనకు లేని వాడు దైవము దూరును,
తనకు గలిగెనేని, దైవమేల?
తనకు దైవమునకు, తగులాటమే* శాంతి. వి. ౮౪
తనదు మనసు చేతఁ దర్కించి జ్యోతిష-
మెంత జేసెనేని నెంచి చూడ,
తన యదృష్టమెల్ల దైవమునకు దెల్సు. వి. ౮౫
తన్నుఁ దెలియు వారు దైవజ్ఞులెంతయు,
నిన్నుఁ దెలియరేని నిలువనేరరి;
మాయఁ దెలియకున్న† మంటి పాలైరయా! వి.

---

83. As the corrupt parts in a sugar-cane must be removed before it can be eaten, so the traitor must be removed from a palace before others can be at ease.

84. When he is in poverty he reproaches Providence: when he has wealth, what does he care about the deity; patience is the proper means of uniting the soul to God.

85. Let a man study astrology as much as he will, his fate is known to God alone.

86. They who know themselves know the Divinity; if they know not thee, they shall never stand; if they know not the true nature of this delusive life, they shall turn to dust.

---

* Al. తగులాటమా which gives no clear meaning.

† A colloquial form, for తెలియకయున్న She is also తెల్సు for తెలుసు in verses 85 and 87.

దైవ - మతుల నరులు తమవంటి వారని,
యరసి గూఢ - తత్వమ' రయ లేరు,
ఇట్లు మాయ పడిన నె' ట్లు మర్మము దెల్సు? వి. ౮౭

నీవు గలుగు చోటు, నెళవు దెలియు వాడు,
వసుధ యందు త్రోవ వదలబో' ందు,
కాలు గదలనీక, గ్రక్కున జేరునో. వి. ౮౮

నీవు నిలిచియుండ, నిఖిలంబు నిలువదు,
నిలిచియుండు నె' ండ - నీరు వలెను;
నీవు నిశ్చయంబు, నిఖిలంబు మాయయు. వి. ౮౯

మొదటన' తడు జ్ఞాన - ముద్రా - ంకితుడు గాక
నా' విధమును' దెలియన' జ్ఞడ' గుచు;
నడుమ జ్ఞానమొ' దవ నగుబాటు ఁగాదయా? వి.

---

87. When men see him who is of heavenly mind, they imagine him to be like themselves, his hidden nature being imperceptible. If thus snared in delusions, how can you learn the secret.*

88. He who knows the abode where Thou dwellest, will walk in no earthly path; his foot shall not stumble, and soon shall he attain.

89. While Thou remainest *eternal*, nothing else shall abide; that which *seems to* last is *fleeting as* the mirage; Thou alone art real, all else is delusion.

90. He who is not originally marked with the seal of wisdom, and remains ignorant of its nature, becomes a fool. It is a jest to suppose that he will in middle life (*between birth and death*) attain to it.

* Compare verse 75.

పికము వనములోన విలసిల్లఁ బలికిన -
భంగి, ప్రాజ్ఞ - జనుల పలుకు గులుకు;
కాకి కూతఁ బోలు, కర్మ - బంధుల కూత. వి. ౯౧

చిక్కి యున్న వేళ సింహంబు నైనను,
బక్క కుక్క సేరి, బాధ సేయు;
బలిమి లేని వేళ, పంతంబు సెల్లదు; వి. ౯౨

జ్ఞానులమని యెంచి చపలాత్ములగు వారు,
తెలివి లేక, తమ్ముఁ దెలియ లేరు,
కష్ట గహనమందు కాడ్పడి యున్నారు. వి. ౯౩

పాప పుణ్యములను పసి - గాపె రుంగునా?
ధరను పరమ యోగి యెరుగు గాక;
లోని పొందికెఁగని లోహముల్ ఁగూర్పరో? వి.

---

91. Sweet as the cuckoo warbling in a garden are the charming words of the wise; but the words of sinners are vile as the cawing of a crow.

92. When even a lion is emaciated, even a starved dog can torment him; when we are powerless all our undertakings are vain.

93. Fickle fools imagine themselves wise, void of understanding, they know not themselves; they are bewildered as in a thick forest.

94. What does a heredsman know of vice and virtue? The perfect sage alone can discriminate them. How can metals be welded unless we know their nature?

పెద్దల వచనములు ప్రేమతోఁ జూచి, తా
నట్టుల నడవఁ బోవ నవ్వు పడదు;
పులిని జూచి నక్క పూఁత బూసిన యట్లు. వి. ౯౫

బుద్ధి-యుతునకేల పొసఁగని సఖ్యంబు?
కార్య వాదికేల కడు చలంబు? *
కుత్సితునకునేల గురు-దేవతా-భక్తి? వి. ౯౬

వినుకరి కనుకరిఁ గోరును,
కనుకరి యాకాంతఁ గూడి, గవయఁగఁ గోరుఁ,
కనుగొన ప్రేమఁ బొరలును
ఘనతర మోహంబు చేటు, గదరా, వేమా. † ౯౭

---

95. He who studies the sayings of the ancient, but fails when he tries to practise *according to them,* is like a fox that streaks itself in *empty imitation of* a tiger.

96. What has he, who is united to wisdom, to do with incongruous friendship? What has he, who speaks to the purpose, to do with circumvention? What has a hypocrite to do with faithfulness to a teacher or a deity?

97. By hearing of her he desires to see her; if he sees her he wishes to possess the maiden; by seeing her he becomes agitated with love: surely strong love is great misery!

---

* For. చ్ఛలం.

† This appears to be translated from a verse of Bhartri Hari
అదర్శనే దర్శనమాత్ర లాలసాః, &c.

ఎల్లి, రేపు, నేడ,' దే' లాగు నైనను,
మనసు నిలుపు వాడు మంచి వాడు,
శివుడు భర్త కర్త ; చింతింపనే' లరా ?   వి.

మరువ వలె పాప-సంగతి
మరువంగా వలెను దురము మఱి విశ్వములో,
మరువ వలె పరుల నేరమిఁ,
మరువంగా వలదు మేలు ; మహిలో వేమా.

ఏమిఁ గొంచు వచ్చెనే' మి దాఁ గొని పోవు?
పుట్టు వేళ నరుడు గిట్టు వేళ ?
ధనములె' చటికే' గు దానే' గునె' చటికి ?   వి.

---

98. He who learns to-day, to-morrow, or the next day to restrain his heart is the best of men ; Siva is the lord and master, why should ye sorrow ?

99. Let us forget every sinful connection ; let us forget every contention and the faults of others ; but never let us forget the good done to us.

100. What did he bring with him into the world when he was born ? and what can he carry with him when he dies ? where shall he go and where will his wealth go ?

కడుపు లోని రోత కడు నోటి యెంగిలి
కడుగ వశమె బ్రహ్మ కొడుకుకైన?
సత్యమున్న కొంత జగతిపై సిద్ధించు. వి. ౧౦౧

ఆశ గోసి వేసి, యనలంబు సల్లార్చి,
గోచి బిగియ గట్టి, కోపము డచి;
యాన విడిచెనేని, యతడు దా యోగిరా. వి.

గుణ - విహీన జనుని, గుణమెంచగానేల?
బుద్ధి లేని వాని పూజ యేమి?
మనసు లేని వాని మంత్రంబులేమయా? వి. ౧౦౩

---

101 The demigods themselves * were not free from the foulness of the belly and spittle in the mouth; but if thou know the truth, it shall render thee victorious.

102. He who has cut off his lusts, and quenched their fire, who has bound his loins, crushed his anger, and given up every desire—this is the *only true* hermit.

103. Why argue about the worth of what is worthless? Why honour him who is devoid of sense? Of what use is a formula Ordained by a fool?

---

* The Hindu moralists very see often waste their satire upon human infirmities, and many verses of a similar tendency have been omitted in the present volume.

కూడు విడిచియు శత - కోటి పడగలెత్తి,
మాటి మాటికి దియు మంట గలిపి,
కాటికే, గు వేళ, కూటికి మోసమై,
దాటి పోదురు జము* దరికి వేమ. ౧౦౪

గీముం† విడిచిపెట్టి, గిక్కురుమ నకుండ,
జీవు విడుచు వేళ శివుని ఁదలచు,
మనసు గొల్పకయును మాయచే బొరలెడు,
పాప - జనులకెచటి పరము వేమ? ౧౦౫

---

104. Those *misers* who strave themselves and place a *dragon's* crest *as a guard* over their treasures ‡ and bury them in the earth ; after *they die and* are burnt shall fall into the hand of Pluto.

105. He who does not resolve to quit his mortal dwelling without a murmur, and to think on the deity when life is departing ; how should he who *at that time* is agitated with uncertainty attain to heaven ?

---

* జముడు యముడు.

† Derive from గృహం a house.

‡ The idea that hidden treasures were guarded by dragon occurs in several Latin authors : in particular Phedrus (Book iv., fable 19). It is also alluded to in the Vicramarca, a Telugu poem, written by Zaccaya, in eight books : this is a work of considerable merits, and parti-

తనకుఁ జేయు మేలు తాఁ దెలియఁగ నేర్చు,
నెలమి తోడ కుక్క యెఱుక భువిని;
తనకు జేయు మేలు, తాఁ దెలియఁగ లేఁడు,
మనుజుఁ డెంత ఖలుఁడు! మహిని వేమ! ౧౦౬

హీన నరుల తోడ, నింతుల తోడను,
పడుచు వాండ్ర తోడ, ప్రభువు తోడ,
ప్రాజ్ఞ జనుల తోడ, బ్రహ్మఘ్న - జనులతో,
వైపు దెలిసి పలుక వలయు వేమ. ౧౦౭

అధిక జనుల తోడ నాప్తుల తోడను,
పరువు గురుతెఱింగి పలుకకున్న,
వచ్చు చెడ్డతనము, హెచ్చుగా గాంభీర్య -
హాని జెందు తనకునప్పుడు, వేమ. ౧౦౮

---

106. A dog instinctively recognizes the kindness shown to it; how base is the man who feels not the good that is done to him.

107. When you talk with the base or with women, with youths or with a ruler, with the wise or with a sacrilegious wretch, be on your guard and speak discreetly.

108. Whether you speak with the great or with your companions respect and consideration are equally necessary, or evil will befall you, and you will lose your respectability.

అరుదుగా నడిగిన యతఁ డర్థి గాఁబోఁడు,
తరుచుగా నొసఁగక, దాత గాఁడు,
దాత కర్థి కింత తారతమ్యము గల్గు. వి.

తల్లి దండ్రు లందు దారిద్ర్యయుతు లందు,
నమ్మిన సిరుపేద నరుల యందు,
ప్రభువు లందు జూఁడ, భయ భక్తు లమరిన,
నిహము పరము గల్గు నెసఁగ వేమ.

“ముట్టు ముట్ట”నుచును “ముట్టరాద” ందురు,
ముట్టుకు దరి యేమి? మూల మేమి?
నవ-బిలముల ముఱికి, నరుల కందరకును,
పుట్టగానె పుట్టు ముట్టు వేమ.

---

109. Occasional requests do not make a ma begger; and he is no benefactor who does not often relieve. There are degrees of more and less between various askers and givers.

110. Our parents, those who are in poverty, the humble dependant who relies on us, and the ruler are to be treated with fear and reverence: this shall gain for us this world and the next.

111. "Thou art defiled and unclean, touch me not," they cry: what limits are there to defilement? what is its source?* all human bodies are equally unclean: defilement is born with ourselves in the body.

---

* That is, Where is the line to be drawn as to what is and what is not defilement.

పరగ తానొసగక పరులు చెప్పిన నైన,
నివ్వజాలక విధినొసగు వాడు,
పొట్టుఁ దినెడి లండి బువ్వలుఁ బెట్టునా. వి. ౧౧౨

అండఁ దప్పిన నరుడతి ధార్మికుని యిల్లు,
ఁజేర వలయు, బ్రతుక జేయునతడు,
ఆవిభీషణునకు నతి గారవంబున,
భూతలమున రాము రీతి, వేమ. వి. ౧౧౩

సకల విద్యఁజూచి, సంతోష పడవచ్చు,
చెయ్యి సాచి, కాసునియ్యలేడు;
చెలగి యొరులకైతె చెప్ప వచ్చును గాని,
తాను జేయ లేడు, ధరను, వేమ. వి. ౧౧౪

---

112. He will bestow nothing on others, though advised to do so; he cannot give, and is inexorable. Will the covetous wretch, who himself lives on bran, give food to others?

113. When a ruined destitute enters the house of a benevolent man, he will be relieved and made to live: such was the conduct of Rama to Vibhishana.*

114. It is easy to feel pleasure in the conversation of the learned; but it is more hard to extend the hand and give a farthing: he can easily advise others to be liberal, but cannot become so himself.

---

* This verse and several others that allude to the incidents in the Ramayana do not resemble the general style of Vemana, and perhaps were not composed by him.

ధర్మ - సత్యములను, దప్పక చేయని,
కర్మ - జీవి మేలు గాన లేడు,
నిర్మల - హృదయుండు నీ* రూపమునను'ండు. వి.

ధనము లేమి కులము తక్కువ పడివచ్చు,
ధనము లేమి కీర్తి (దలగి పోవు;
ధనము లేమి శుచిని దగ బుట్టని య్యదు,
ధనము లేమి ఘనత దప్పు, వేమ. ౧౧౬

ధనము - లేమి, సుతులు తప్పుల (బెడుదురు,
ధనము లేమి పత్ని దాకనాడు;
ధనము లేమె' వరికి తాళికై యుండదు. వి. ౧౧౭

చచ్చు వారలె' వరు? చావని వా రే రి?
చచ్చి బ్రతికి యుండు, జనము లె' వరు;
విచ్చలవిడిగా† ను, వివరించి చూడ రా. వి. ౧౧౮

115. The evil heart that departs from uprightness and truth shall never see any good. He that is pure of heart shall be converted into Thy form.

116. By want of wealth even caste becomes degraded; all fame is blotted out by want of wealth; poverty leads to the loss of purity, and puts an end to respectability.

117. When a man becomes poor, his very sons find fault with him; when he loses his fortune, his wife upbraids him; a poor man is thought utterly intolerable.

118. Who are those that die? who are the immortal? who are those who participate both in death and immortality? Judge freely and perceive the truth: *the body perishes, but the soul survives.*

* నీరూపం substituted for నిజరూపం "own form," which is obscure.

† విచ్చలవిడి appears to be derived from యథేచ్ఛ to which it is equivalent.

బ్రతుకు వారలె' వరు, బ్రతుకకు'ందురె' వరు,
బ్రతికి బ్రతుకు లేని, ప్రాణు లె' వరు?
క్షితిని శోధఁజేసి, స్థిరముగఁజూడరా. వి. ౧౧౯

పెట్టు వారలె' వరు? పెట్టకు'ందురె' వరు?
పెట్టి పెట్టన'ట్టి దిట్ట లె' వరు?
పట్టు దప్పకు'ండ, భావించి చూడరా. వి. ౧౨౦

పుట్టు వారలె' వరు? పుట్టకు'ందురె' వరు?
పుట్టి పుట్టన'ట్టి, పురుషులె' వరు?
పుట్టి పుట్టని యట్టు, బోధించి చూడరా. వి. ౧౨౧

కట్టు వారలె' వరు? కట్టని వారే' రి?
కట్టి కట్టు లేని కర్తలె' వరు?
గట్టిపరచి, లెస్స కనుకల్గి చూడరా. వి. ౧౨౨

---

119. Who are those who live? who are they who live not (*to any useful purpose*)? which are they (*inanimate beings*) which can neither be said to live or the contrary. Inquire and examine of these.

120. Who are the liberal and the illiberal? who is the inexorable *miser* that will not effectually relive the poor? consider and know this without erring.

121. Who are the born and the unborn? what are those that are born and those that are unborn?* discern well that which is born and that which is not born.

122. Who are those that bind and bind not? who are the fools who neither preserve nor preserve not: have eyes and discern this.

* The body and the spirit.

ఇట్టి పద్య - పంచకై' ష్యముఁ దెలిసిన,
పెట్టి, పుట్టి, కట్టి, పృథివి బ్రతికి,
చచ్చి, శుద్ధుఁడ' గుచు, సర్వజ్ఞుఁడై, నిల్చు
నె' ల్ల మహిమ నీకుఁ జెల్లు వేమ. ౧౨౩

ముక్కు కోపములును, మోహ - లోభంబులు,
*న' క్కజంపు క్రూరమ' ధికమ' య్యె ;
కక్కసంబు సేత కాలుని చేతను,
మొక్కఁ బోదురు తుది, మొనసి వేమ. ౧౨౪

చిత్తము గల యోగి శివుని వలెనె యుండు,
మిథ్య - యోగి యుండు మిడత వలెను,
నిత్యుఁడై' నయోగి నీవలెను' ండురా. వి. ౧౨౫

---

123. He who knows the fruit † of these five verses, who aids, is born, stores up, lives, and dies, shall be wise and perfect.

124. Those who have anger in the nostrils,* with desire and avarice in excess, shall, through prodigious cruelty, and through harsh conduct, fall into the hand of Pluto and perish.

125. The saint who posesses a *religious* heart shall shine as a god, but the hypocrite shall perish as a grasshopper ; the steadfast saint will resemble Thee.

---

† *Panchaca*, a collection of five, *aishgam*, the future result. These verses have been preserved as characteristic of the author, rather than for their intrinsic value. The mystic meaning is explained in several ways. In the book of *Proverbs* (particularly chap. xxx.) we meet with several passages written in this style.

* Rash, fury ; అక్కజం is derived from ఆశ్చర్యం and కక్కసం, from కర్కశం.

ఉన్న సరికి మనుజుఁడు పకారి గాలేక,
కన్ను గనక నెల్ల గర్వములను,
దీనులైన వారి దిగువాయిగాఁ జూచి,
పరము గనక నూతఁ బడును, వేమ. ౧౨౬
రోగియైన వాఁడు రోగినెఱుంగును;
రోగినరసి చూచి రూఢి గాను,
రోగికిడిన వాని, రాగి బంగారౌను. వి. ౧౨౭
ఎదుటి తన బలంబు నెంచుకో నేరక,
దీకొని చలమున నెదిర్చెనేని,
ఎలుగు పంజు సేవ కేర్పడు చందమా. వి. ౧౨౮
ఓగు బాగెఱుగని యొట్టి మూఢ - జనంబు
లెల సుధీ - జనముల నెంచు టెల్ల,
మృగపు* తోడ, కుక్క మొఱగిన సామ్యమా. వి.

---

126. If a man in this life be not a doer of good; if through pride he cannot see with his eyes—if he look upon the poor man as beneath him, he shall never see heaven, but shall fall into the pit.

127. The sick man feels for the sick; and verily when he views the patient, the copper he gives him shall turn to gold.

128. If, ignorant of his own powers, and those of his opponent a man blusters and indulges in wrath, he is like a bear performing the torch dance, *in which he will of course be burnt.*

129. A fool who knows not rights from wrong, if he passes a judgment upon wise men, is like a dog barking against a lion.

---

* *Mriga-pa* the lord of animals, the lion.

నేరని జనులకును నేర్పు నేరములెల్ల,
చక్కఁజేతురరయ సాధు జనము,
లోప్పు దుర్జనములు తప్పుగనెంతురు. వి. ౧౩౦
దిక్కు లేని రోగి, దీనతఁబాపిన;
పురుషుఁడిహము నందు పూజ్యుఁడగును;
పరమునందు వాని భాగ్యమేమనవచ్చు? * వి.
పలుగు వానికేల పర - సమృద్ధిఁదలంప?
పలుగు వానికేల భక్తి పథము?
పలుగు వానికేల పరమార్థ - తత్వంబు. వి. ౧౩౨
తండ్రి సొమ్మునైన, దాయాది సొమ్మైన,
పరుల సొమ్ములైన, ప్రాప్త - ధనము
దయను దీనులకును దానమిచ్చిన వాఁడె
బహుళ - పుణ్య - జనుడు; పరగ వేమ. ౧౩౩

---

130. The good man will correct the errors and omissions of the ignorant, while the wicked man finds fault even with what is right.

131. The man who relieves the poverty of the sick and destitute shall be honored even in this life: but who can tell the happiness he shall enjoy in the next world?

132. What does the miscreant care for relieving others? Can the sinner ever attain to the path of faith? What can a wicked wretch know of spiritual truth?

133. Whether his wealth be derived from the estate of his father, from a relation, or from any others—he alone can be considered virtuous who freely and affectionately bestows it on the poor.

---

*One manuscript adds జీవినరయు, జీవి శివుడు వేమ,

తనదు సొమ్ము (జూడ, దానమియ్యగ వచ్చు,
నవని దొడ్డ గాదె వరికైన,
నదరు బెదురు లేక నన్యుల సొమ్ముల
దానమిచ్చు వాడు దాత వేమ. ౧౩౪

ధైర్య-యుతునకితర ధనమైన నదురేమి?
దానమిచ్చునపుడె తనకు దక్కు,
నెలమి మించు పనికి నెవరేమి సేయుదు
రడుగు దప్ప తప్పు పిడుగు వేమ. ౧౩౫

ద్రోహ బుద్ధినైన దొంగరికమునైన,
సటలనైన సాహసమునైన,
సంపదధిక చేత, సాధించి ధనమును,
బడుగుకిచ్చి, బాగు పడును, వేమ. ౧౩౬

---

134. Every man may give of his own, and this is no great matter to any one; he alone can be called liberal who without hesitation takes the property of others and bestows it in gifts.*

135. Why should a man of resolution hesitate because the property belongs to another? By bestowing it in charity it becomes his own: what can be done to him? the thunderbolt falls *innocuous* at his feet.

136. Whatever riches have been accumulated either by evil devices, by theft, by fraud, or by any rash act;† whoever has hereby become rich, shall still be happy if he bestows much on the poor.

* The principle inculcated in this and the next verses is also found in the laws of Manu. Vemana perhaps is not the author of these passages.

† Sahasam; impetuosity, rashness, imprudence.

నరుడ' టు పరమా' త్మ గురుని ఁజేరిన' పుడ,
హస్తమ' ందు మోక్షమ' పుడె చూపు,
విరివి - సంపదలను విర్ర వీగిన జీవి,
పరమె' రుగక యముని పాలు వేమ. ౧౩౭

బిడ్డలను, సతులను, పేరైన చుట్టాల
సంపదల, తనువుల, ఁజాల నమ్మి,
సంతసిల్లుచుం' డు క్షణభంగురముల' న్ని'
తెలియ లేర' దే' మి దెల్ప వేమ. ౧౩౮

ఉచితవంతుడై' నను' ద్యోగ - పరుడైన,
సాగిపారి యున్న సమయమునను,
పరులకు' పకరించి పరగ రక్షించును. * వి. ౧౩౯

137. When a man has found a superior spiritual teacher, he shall show him happiness, *as distinctly as though it were* in the palm of his hand : but the creature that is puffed up with abundant wealth shall never know happiness ; he shall fall into the hand of Pluto.

138. They who have children, wives, and great relations ; who rely much on their possessions and their *mortal* bodies, delighting in them, but all are momentarily perishable ; they know it not : who can teach this to them ?

139. If a prudent man is in any honorable employment, let him, while he is in prosperity, do good to others and relieve his neighbours.

* One MS. adds శాశ్వతి సిద్ధి చేత వసర వేమ

పట్టు వస్త్రములును, పరగ భూషణములు,
కుదువబె' ట్టుటె' ల్ల కొదువపద్దు
ల' నుభవింప కూడద' తడె' ంత వాడైన
న' నుభవింప కొంత హాని వేమ. ౧౪౦:

మని యుండెడు జనమె' ల్లను,
* చని - పోయిన - వారి పుణ్య - సత్కథలె' లమిగా,
వినవలె, కనవలె, మనవలె
†న, నిమిషులకునై' న (దెలియద' ంత్యము వేమా.

---

140. It is a very base act to pawn silken vestments or jewels ; no man whatever ought to use such *pledges* ; if used, they are in a certain degree injured.‡

141. Let us listen to the histories of those who have lived of old ; and attentively read the holy legends* regarding those who are dead : let us live accordingly: the gods themselves know not what shall hereafter happen.

---

* *Punya catha* : a legend the perusal of which is a *meritorious* act.

† *Animish* ; a god ; literally, one whose eyelids do not move. The gods are represented by statues or pictures, the eyelids of which are of course fixed ; and this name I imagine to originate in that circumstance.

‡ Several verses of a similar tendency are here omitted, as they appear to be spurious. The present one seems to be translated from the Digest of Hindu Law, part I., chap. II., section LX. See Colebrooke's Translation, vol. I. p. 1 09.

*పచ్చ (జూచువారు, పచ్చ మెచ్చెడు వారు,
పచ్చ మీాద వాంఛ పడిన వారు,
పచ్చ విడుచు వాని ప్రభువుగా (జూతురు. వి. ౧౪౨

ప్రస్తుతంపు వేళ పద్యంబు చదివిన,
తప్పు (గలిగి యున్న నొప్పి యుండు,
వెలది సురత వేళ బిత్తలై యుండదా. వి. ౧౪౩

బంగరు (బోడగన్న, భామల (బోడగన్న,
చిత్తమునను చింత సేయడేని
వాడె పరమ - యోగి వర్ణింప జగమందు. వి.

---

142. Those who enjoy wealth,* those who laud it, and those who long for it, look upon him as a superior who abstains from it.

143. If the song suit the occasion, however incorrect, it is acceptable. † *Where love exists, ornament is superfluous.*

144. He who can look upon gold and upon the charms of women with equal indifference, shall be praised as the most perfect of men.

---

* The word pacca, literally *yellow*, is said to be sometimes used for gold; but the present verse is the only instance in which I have met with it. Compare verse 148.

† This verse appears to be translated from the following, by Pandita Rayalu :—

అవసర పఠితాவாணீ
గుణగణరహితాపి వహతి పరమోదం
రతిసమయే యువతీనాం
భూషాహానిశ్చ భూషణం భవతి.

In the third line, బిత్తలి *naked* is often written బిత్తరి which signifies *blooming*. The former word is nearly peculiar to the western districts.

పతి యొప్పిన సతియొప్పును,
పతి సతులొక్కటైన పరమ - పావనమందుర్,
సతి పతి న్యాయమె మోక్షం
బతులిత పరమాత్మయైక్యము గురా! వేమా. ౧౪౫
ఆకాశంబున వాయువు,
మ్రాకున దావాగ్నియటుల, మానసమందున్,
యేకా, కారుడు, జగమున,
జోకై తనుఁ దాని వెల్గు, సుమ్మిర, వేమా. ౧౪౬
కండ - కావరమున కానరు మరణంబు,
తను మదమునఁ గనడు, తత్వమిట్లు,
భోగ - వాంఛ చేత, పుణ్యంబు గానడు. వి. ౧౪౭

---

145. If the wife delights in what pleases her husband, and if the married pair are united as one, this leads to perfect purity. The duties of man and wife *lead to* deliverance *from sin*; this shall form a means whereby they shall be united to the great spirit, *that is of* incomparable *perfection.**

146. *Imperceptible* as air in the sky, and fire in wood, does the first of beings freely pervade the world, and shine independent of others. †

147. By reason of the stoutness of his body he trusts that he shall never see death; through fatness of flesh he fails of seeing the truth; by attachment to pleasure he can see no holiness.

---

* The great obscurity of this verse requires a paraphrastic translation.

† This principle has been exhibited in many forms in the present author.

Deusest, quodeunque vides, quocunque mover is.

తెలుపు మాపు (జేసి, దిట్ట-తనంబున,
తెలుపు భస్మముగను తేట-పరచు
విధముకన్న పరుస వేదియు లేదురా! వి. ౧౪౮

దుండగీనికో'కడు, కొండీడు చెలికాడు,
బాడ రాజునకును బడుచు మంత్రి,
కొండముచ్చునకును కోతియువిందౌను. వి. ౧౪౯

పుట్టు దుఃఖముననను, పొరలు దుఃఖముననను,
గిట్టు దుఃఖముననను, క్రిద జనును,
మనుజ-దుఃఖము వలె మరి లేదు దుఃఖంబు. వి.

పెట్టిన'ంత ఫలము పెక్కుండ్రకు, పహతి
జేయకు'న్న దాను జెరుపకు'న్న,
పెండ్లి సేయున'ట్టి పెద్ద ఫలంబురా. వి. ౧౫౧

---

148. If you kill quicksilver* and burn it thoroughly, and purify it, there is no better mode of discovering the philosopher's stone.

149. The talebearer is the associate of the villain; a stripling is a fit minister for an inflexible king; and the monkey is the only companion for the baboon.

150. He is born in sorrow and lives in sorrow: he dies in sorrow and goes down *to* the grave: surely there is no grief greater than that suffered by man.

151. To refrain from grieving others is as meritorious as sustaining the poor: and to keep from injuring men is as good a deed as marriage.

---

* *Telupu* literally is whiteness; compare verse 142: several more verses on similar subjects are here omitted. For తేట we might better read దిట్టపరచి to rectify.

మేక చంకఁబెట్టి మెలగుచు, మందలోఁ,
భ్రమసి తిరుగు గొల్ల పగిది గాక,
దైవమె'రుగక పెర దైవతముల దల్చు. వి. ౧౫౨

వెర్రి బట్టు వాని వినయంబుల'ధికంబు,
చెడ్డ ముఁడ ముసుగు చెలగి పెట్టు,
చెడిపె *కొఁడుకు మిగుల ఁజేయునా'చారంబు. వి.

పర - ధనములకు చెయి పట్టెను మిక్కిలి,
సత్యమి'ంత లేక జారుడ'య్యె,
ద్విజుడ'నఁగొను దాను తేజమి'ంతయు లేక. వి.

ఇమ్ము ఁదప్పు వేళ నె'మ్మెల'న్నియు దప్పి,
కాల మొ'క్క రీతి గడుప వలయు,
విజయుడ'నుగు ఁదప్పి విరటుని గొలువడా. వి. ౧౫౫

---

152. Those who roam *to other lands in pilgrimage* to find the God that dwells within them are like a shepherd who searches in his flock for the sheep he has under his arm.

153. Who behaves himself more cautiously than a madman? who assumes more modest airs than a poor widow? and who is so strict in religious rites as the worthless?

154. He constantly stretches out his hand to seize his neighbour's wealth, and devoid of all truth he becomes a roving debauchee. So entirely worthless he still calls himself twiceborn!

155. If you have missed your opportunity, it is best to lay aside all pretences, and pass your time privately. Did not Arjuna, when unsuccessful, enter into the service of Virata? †

* Al. చేడె

† An allusion to a in the Mahabharata.

మెలతన' డవిను' ంచి, మృగము వెఁటనె పోవు
రామ - చంద్రుకన్న రసికు డే' డి?
చేటు కాలమునకు చెడు బుద్ధి పుట్టును. వి. ౧౫౬

లంక బోవు నాడు లంకా' ధి - పతి రాజ్య
మ' ంత కీశ - సేనలా' క్రమించె,
చేటు కాలమైన చెరపన' ల్పుడుఁ జాలు. వి. ౧౫౭

రామ - విభుడు పుట్టి - రఘు - కులంబ' లరించె;
కురు - విభుండు పుట్టి కులము జెరిచె,
యెవరి మంచి చెడ్డ లె' ంచి, చూచిన తేట. వి.

---

156. Rama left his spouse at home, and went to seek the antelope *sent to delude him!* Yet where is there one of sounder judgment than Rama? in the time of misforturne a man is subject to such temptations!

157. On the day when Lanca fell, the kingdom was plundered by an army of apes! When one is in ill luck, the weakest foe is sufficient to destroy us!

158. The race of Raghu was prosperous in consequence of the birth of Rama therein, while the birth of Duryodhana ruined his entire tribe. The causes of all good and evil in a family are easily perceived.

పుర హరునకు నేత పురువు * తానేసిన,
స్థిరము గల్గు జ్ఞాన జీవమయ్యె,
నేతకేమి వచ్చె నిజ - భక్తి హేతువు. వి. ౧౫౯

శుద్ధ - దృష్టిఁ దెలిసి, శుక్రుఁడంతటి వాఁడు,
పట్టలేక మనసు పార విడిచి,
కన్నుఁబోయి పిదప కాకి చందంబయ్యె. వి. ౧౬౦

పంచా - క్షరి బీజంబుల
నంచితముగనెఱుఁగునాఁతఁడఖిలజ్ఞుండై,
వంచనమెఱుగక కువలయ
సంచారము సేయునతఁడు శంభుఁడు వేమా. ౧౬౧

---

159. The spider that wove its web over Siva *to conceal him when he fled* was rewarded with superior instinct: yet of what avail was its worthless weaving? Faith will render any work acceptable.

160. Even so clear-sighted a sage as Sucrachari, by failing to restrain his curiosity, lost an eye, and was reduced to the condition of a crow. †

161. He who truly knows the name that contains five syllables ‡ shall become all wise; he shall never know dishonor, and, while walking in this earth, shall be changed into the deity.

---

*For పురుగు. In many Telugu words g is Commutable into v. So పాదిగి, పాదివి, పగలు, పవలు, తీగ, తీవ, అగుట, అవుట, &c.

† The legends here referred to occur in the Bhagavata and the Ramayana. From its particular action when looking at any object, the crow is imagined by the Hindus to have but one eye.

‡ This is the name *Namasivaya,* one of the most scared titles of the Supreme Being.

శూద్రులందు బుట్టి, శూద్రుల దూషించి,
ద్విజులమ' నెడు పేరు నిజము ఁజేసి,
మనసు నిల్పకున్న మరి శూద్రుఁడ' ధముఁడు. వి.

నొసలు బత్తుడ' య్యె, నోరు తోడేల' య్యె,
మనసు భూతము వలె మలయుగాను,
"శివుని గనియెన" న్న సిగ్గె' ట్లు గాద' కో! వి. ౧౬౩

మాదిగ చెయువులను మనసులో బెట్టుక,
మాదిగెలను దెగడు మాదిగె' పుడు
మంచి గుణము లేక మరి ద్విజుడెట్లగు? వి. ౧౬౪

---

162. They whe are born Sudras, and yet revile Sudras; who hold themselves twice born, and rely on that title; still, if unable to restrain their hearts, are the lowest of Sudras. *

163. His forehead † is that of a worshipper; his mouth that of a wolf; and his heart that of a roaming demon: is he so shameless as to say he has learnt of the divinity?

164. If a man still has in his heart the principles of a Pariar, and yet scorns Parias, how should he become twiceborn while devoid of every good quality?

---

* Every son of a Bramin is considered a Sudra until the ceremony of upanayanam is performed, whereby children are introduced into the caste.

† Alluding to the sectarial mark worn on the forehead.

కల్లలా' డు కంటె కష్టంబు మరియును,
కష్టమె' పుడునో' లి గలిగి యుండు
ద్విజుడన' నుట చూడ దిమ్మరితనమ' ది. వి. ౧౬౫

విప్ర వరులమ' నుచు, వేదంబు జదువుచు,
ప్రాకృతులను జూచి పరిహాసించు,
ధరణి-సురలకన్న దాసరి మతమె' చ్చు, వి. ౧౬౬

వేషమొ' నర గట్టి వెలయ శూద్రత్వంబు
తనకు లేద' నుకొను ధరణి ద్విజుడు *
అరిది గిట్టు వేళన' డగు ద్విజత్వంబు. వి. ౧౬౭

---

165. There is no sin greater than that of falsehood: this is an abomination perpetually † in the mouth: what vagabonds are several who call themselves twice-born!

166. The lords of the earth ‡ say, "We are pure; we are learned in the scriptures;" they scorn all who are in their natural state. Truly the poorest palmer is better than such boasters.

167. The Brahmin, when he has assumed a particular garb, imagines he is no Sudra: is it not strange that his braminhood perishes when he dies?

---

* This elision is here unnecessary. See the Grammar of Nannaya Bhatt Section fix.

† ఓలి *oli* or ఒగి *ogi*: these two words are mere expletives to fill the metre; they are sometimes explained *duly*, *Always*.

‡ That is, Brahmins who have this title.

సోమ యాజిన నుచు సొంపుతో వేషంబు,
గట్టి మాంసమెల్ల గాల్చి తినును,
ద్విజుడనే న నగన ధిక మేమి తనవల్ల. వి. ౧౬౮

అంతరా-త్మ గనక న ల్ప-బుద్ధుల తోడ,
మెలగెడు ద్విజులెల్ల మేదిన ందు,
యముని నరకములకున రుగంగని ది సాక్షి. వి.

కల్ల టికెకుభూతి గట్టిగా పెట్టిన
న ందులోని కంపుల డగన ట్లు,
మెడను త్రాడు వ్రేసి మెరుపుతో ద్విజుడౌ నె? వి.

---

168. You call yourself a Somayaji * and wear a particular dress: why? because you have roasted and eaten flesh! what are you the better for calling yourself a Bramin?

169. Those who imagine themselves twice-born so walk as proves them unable, through their light minds, to see the hidden spirit. This is a witness that they are going to the realm of Pluto.

170. Will the application of white ashes † do away the smell of a winepot? Will a cord cast over your neck make you twice born.

---

* One who has performed the *yagnya* sacrifice is thus styled; at that ceremony a goat is roasted, and every Bramin who assists in the rite is obliged to eat of the flesh.

† Alluding to the white ashes (called vibhuti) with which Bramins and others paint their bodies. The cord here mentioned is the braminical thread.

చీంచు రక్తములను, జెరసి న దేహంబు,
చందమె' రుగక ద్విజ-శబ్దమి' డుక,
నడచినను విడుచునొ నరకంబు మృత్యువు. వి. ౧౭౧

భూతి దేహమ' ందు బూసి తేనా యనా?
నిష్ఠ శివుని యందు నిలుప వలయు,
గాక భస్మమ' ందు గాడిదె పొర్లదా? వి. ౧౭౨

ఆకులె' ల్లఁ దిన్న మేక-పోతులకె' ల్ల,
గాక పోయెన' య్యె కాయ-సిద్ధి,
లోకులె' ల్ల వెఱ్ఱిపోకిళ్ళఁ బోదురు. వి. ౧౭౩

బోడి-తలలు, జడలు, బూడిదె పూతలా,
భాషణా' సనములు, వేషములను,
యోగి గాఁడు, లోన బాగు గాకు' ండెనా. వి.

---

171. If he forget the nature of his body which is composed *of flesh and blood*, and pride himself on the title of "twice-born," will death and hell hereby lose their power over him?

172. What are you the better for smearing your body with *sacred* ashes? your thoughts should be set on God alone; otherwise an ass can wallow in dirt as well as you!

173. Even a goat can attain to such "corporeal perfection"* as consists in living on leaves: how apt men are to fall into foolish whims!

174. Bald heads! matted locks! daubing with ashes, harangues, postures, and a religious garb! No man is a saint who is not pure within.

---

* The technical term for the state to which those hope to attain who live in forests as hermits.

వేష భాషలె' ఱిగి కాషాయ - వస్త్రముల్,
బోడి - నెత్తి గల్గి బొరయుచు' ండ్రు;
తలలు బోడులై' న, తలపులు బోడులా? వి. ౧౭౫
కాలు సేయి వంచి, గాలి నిండగ (జేర్చి,
నేల ప్రాలి కొన్ని, నిలిచి కొన్ని,
యాసన ముఖ విద్యల, భ్యాస విద్యలు. వి. ౧౭౬
కావి - పంచె గట్టి, కడు యోగి వలెను' ండి,
వెలికి గోర్కు-లె' ల్ల విడిచి పెట్టి,
తోడరి తిరుగు వాడు, దొంగ సన్యాస యా. వి.
కలి - యుగమున బుట్టి, కడతేరగా లేక,
యొడలు బడల జేసి యుగ్ర తపము,
తమరు చేసి యేమి, తత్వంబు (గన లేరు. వి. ౧౭౮

---

175. *Sanyasis* acquaint themselves with particular words and vests; they wear a brick-red garb and shaven pates; on these they pride themselves; their heads look very pure, but are their hearts so?

176. You bend your legs and arms *according to rule*, and fill your bodies with air, *holding your breath;* sometimes crawling and again standing. The religious postures are mere tricks that are learnt.

177. He who assumes a tinted cloak and imitates great hermits, laying aside every external wish, he who pretends to walk this is the hypocritical *Sanyasi*!

178. The sons of this iron age* are unable to attain to heaven; they vex their bodies with austere penance! why? they are ignorant of the truth.

---

* Cali yuga.

ఇల్లునా' లు విడిచి యినుప కచ్చులఁగట్టి,
వంటకంబు నీరు వాంఛలు' డిగి,
వంటినున్న యంత వచ్చునా తత్వంబు? వి. ౧౭౯

జీవ_లింగ పూజ సేసిన వారికి,
శిలల రూపము' ందు చింత యేల?
చెలగి మధువు గ్రోలి* చేదు రుచించునా? వి.

శివుడు గలడ' టంచు శిలలకు మ్రొక్కెటి,
వెఱ్ఱి జీవులార వెతల విడుడి;
జీవుల' ందె కాక శిలల నేము' న్నది? వి. ౧౮౧

రాతి ప్రతిమఁదెచ్చి రాజసంబున నుంచి,
పూజ సేయు నరుడు బుద్ధి మాలి,
భావము' ందు పరము భావించ నేరడో! వి. ౧౮౨

---

179. If he leaves his house and his wife, binds his loins with iron, and gives up all inclinations for meal and drink, if he chooses to live in solitude, will this gain him heaven?

180. How should those who adore the living principle † still honor images made of stone? who that has tasted honey will again taste poison.

181. O ye senseless creatures, who bow down to stones imagining that the deity exists therein! cease from these ideas: it may be in living beings, but what is there in a stone?

182. A man makes a stone image, and sets it up in dignity, and worships it! he is devoid of sense. He cannot comprehend the deity that dwells within him!

---

* Al. చెలగి చెక్కెరతిని.

† *Lingam*: Literally, a feature, characteristic or discriminative mark such as that of gender. Metaphorically a *principle* of nature or belief.

జంగమా' ఖ్య, భక్తి సంధి, వేరే లేదు;
సగుణ - భావమి' దియు, శాస్త్ర - విధియు,
నిర్గుణంబు వీడు, నెరవే' ది యెరుగడు. వి. ౧౮౩

ఎంబెరు మతమ'ందు నె' సగి మాంసముదిని,
మారు పేర్లు పెట్టి, మధువు ద్రావి,
వావి వరుసఁ దప్పి వలికి పాలౌ' దురు. వి. ౧౮౪

జాతి మతము విడిచి, చని, యోగిగా మేలు,
జాతి తోనె యున్న నీతు లే' ల?
మతము బట్టి జాతి మానకు' ంటకొరత? వి. ౧౮౫

---

183. The *term* "Zangam" is a *mere* denomination: faith forms the tie (*between him and the deity*)—no more. It is a qualified state of being: this is the tenet ordained *for our belief*. This man has erred: he knows not the inscrutable.*

184. Those who embrace the Embari † sect eat flesh, change their names and drink wine: they transgress the lines of consanguinity and become the portion of the grave.

185. It is good to forsake tribe and caste and become a hermit: what is the good of instruction so long as you retain your caste? It is base, after embracing a creed, to hesitate about giving up caste.

---

* This and a few other verses are allowed a place in the present volume, as specimens of the mystic theories inculculated by this writer, and admired by those who imagine them intelligible.

† Or Satani: one species of dissenters from the common faith of the Hindus.

కట్టె పేరులొడఁ గట్టిచెప్పఁగ రాదు,
కాన రాదు లోని కలితనంబు,
జంగమైన పిదప జాతినెంచఁగ రాదు. వి. ౧౮౬
వేద - విద్యలెల్ల వేశ్యల వంటివి,
భ్రమల బెట్టి తేటపడఁగనీయవు,
గుప్త - విద్యయొకటి కుల - కాంత వంటిది. వి.
వేద - శాస్త్రములను విననేమి గుడిచిరి,
యరిది తిరిగి చత్తురందరిండ్లు,
బ్రహ్మ మహిమఁ దెలిసి బ్రతుకుట నిజముగా! వి.
వ్రతములెన్ని యైన వట్టి చిక్కులె కాని,
యాత్మ చిక్కు గాననలవి గాదు,
ఆత్మ చిక్కు బాపునతఁడె పో ఘన - యోగి. వి.

---

186. As pieces of wood of *various kinds*, when formed into a ship, *are no longer distinguished by their names and* their interior qualities are undistinguished; so after entering the Zangam sect, a man's *former* caste is forgotten.

187. The books that are called the Vedas are like courtezans, deluding men, and wholly unintelligible; but the hidden knowledge of God, is like an honourable wife.

188. What are you the better for listening to the Vedas and Sastras? you roam from house to house, and then die. Learn the greatness of God, and verily you shall live.

189. Your religious rites, however numerous, are mere entanglements : these give you no power to loose the bondage of the soul. He alone is a saint who has obtained freedom.

జనన - మరణములను, సంధ్య, త్రాడును లేదు,
సంధ్య త్రాడు లేదు, జననికె' పుడు,
తల్లి శూద్రురాలు తానె' ట్లు బాపడు. వి. ౧౯౦.

పితర యన్నమ' నుచు, బ్రీతితో బిలిపించి,
కాకులకును బెట్టు కర్మలార!
కాకుల' ందునే' మి ఘనులకు బెట్టుడీ. వి. ౧౯౧.

పిండములను జేసి పితరుల ఁదలపోసి,
కాకులకును బెట్టు గాడ్దెలార,
పియ్యి దినెడు కాకి పితర మెట్లాగయా? వి. ౧౯౨.

---

190. The daily prayers and the braminical cord are wanting both at birth and at the time of death: his mother never enjoyed either of these; and if his mother be a Sudra, how can he be a Brahmin? *

191. You call it "food for your ancestors," but you call the crows together, with all kindness, and give it to them, ye formal professors! what is the good of charity to crows? give rather to good men?

192. O ye asses! why do you make balls of food and give them to the crows in the name of your ancestors? How can a dung-eating crow be an ancestor of yours?

---

* The ceremony of upanayanam is never performed upon female children of Brahmins, who thus are, says Vemana no better than Sudras.

నల్ల బోడి తలలు, తెల్లని గొంగళ్లు
నొ' డల బూడ్దె - పూత, యొంటి - రోత !
యిట్టి వేషములును పొట్ట కోసమె సుమీ. వి.
కంబళములు గట్టి గంతలు గజ్జెలు,
బోడి - తలలు కావి బొరయు చీర
లా' త్మ - దేవ * పూజ ల' వి సేయ నేరవు. వి. ౧౯౪
మానసపు విరక్తి మసలక నా' త్మలో,
బోడి తలల సొంపు పొల్పు మీర,
కడుపు కొరకుఁ దిరుగు కష్టంపు మతి తోడ. వి.
పుస్తకములు, జడలు, పులితోలు, బెత్తంబు,
కక్షపాలలు, పది - లక్షలై' న,
మోత చేటు గాని మోక్షంబు లేదయా. వి. ౧౯౬

193. Shaven heads, and a dress of white woollen, smearing with ashes, and disgusting bodies ! Truly such habiliments are used for the sake of the belly alone !

194. A rug, bells, anclets, bald pates, and a dyed vest ! these are insufficient for the worship of God who is a spirit.

195 He who walks not in self-denial in his heart, and only prides himself on the grace of a shaven head, lives for the sake of his belly, with an evil mind.

196. A breviary, matted locks, a tiger skin, a staff, a reliquary, † and so forth ; he merely has the trouble of carrying these about ; they can never effect his salvation.

* Al. ఆత్మ - లింగ - పూజ.

† More literally, a pouch or knapsack wherein the implements used in worship are carried about. "*And so forth*" lit. *for ten lacks.*

హృదయము పదిలంబై తే,
గుదిగొను సన్యాసమునకు కొమ్ములు గలవా?
యిది యెరుగరు చదువరులు,
మది ముక్తికి నాస్పదంబు మహిలో వేమా. ౧౯౭

ఆసనముల బన్ని, యంగంబు బిగియించి,
యొడలు విరుచుకొనెడు యోగమెల్ల,
జెట్టి సాము కన్న చింతాకు తక్కువ. వి. ౧౯౮

కడుపు బోరగించి, కన్నులు ముకుళించి, *
బిర్ర బిగుసుకున్న బీద - యోగి,
యముని బారి గొర్రె యతడేమి సేయును? వి.

---

197. If they heart be set aright, what is the good* of regular ordination as a monk. Scholars are ignorant of this, that the heart is the only basis of salvation.

198. Religion that consists in contriving various postures and twisting the limbs is just one straw inferior to the exercises of the wrestler.

199. The wretched ascetic pushes out his belly, winks his eyes, and strains with all his body! He is like a sheep bound for sacrifice, and no better!

---

* Al. చీకిరించి "blinking with the eyes!" contracted, for the sake of the metre into చీక్రించి.

† Lit. *Has a hermit horns?* Horns being considered, as among the Jews, marks of power or dignity.

రేచక, పూరక, కుంభక,
సూచకముల రాజ-యోగి సుస్థిర మతియై,
లో చూపు జూడనొ ల్లక,
వాచా బ్రహ్మంబు పలుక వద్దుర వేమా. ౨౦౦

పడి పడి మ్రొక్కఁగనే టికి,
గుడి-లోపల కఠిన శిలల గుణములు చెడునా?
గుడి దేహమా త్మ దేవుఁడు,
చెడు-రాళ్లకు వట్టి పూజ సేతురు వేమా! ౨౦౧

పలుగు రాళ్లఁ దెచ్చి, పరగ గుడుల గట్టి,
చెలఁగి శిలల సేవ జేయనే ల?
శిలల సేవఁ జేయ, ఫలమే మి గల్గురా? వి. ౨౦౨

---

200. Be not like those haughty monks who imagine that by *the gestures appointed for* respiration, inspiration, and retention of the breath, they have attained to wisdom. In the absence of inward vision boast not of mere oral divinity.

201. Why bow and fall down *in worship*? will the hard stone in the temple change its nature? The true temple is the body, the soul is the god therein; empty is the worship ye pay to these worthless stone.

202. Why collect *slabs of* marble, build temples with them, and delight to worship stones? What profit have you of adoring a stone?

ఉపవసములను' న్ననూ' ర - పంద్దై పుట్టు;
తపసియై దరిద్రతను వహించు,
శిలకు మ్రొక్కన' గును జీవము' డుగు బొమ్మ. వి.

ఇహము విడిచి ఫలముల' ంపుగ గలవ' ని,
వహించి బల్కు వారి మతము కల్ల,
ఇహము లోన బరముని' సగుట గానరో. వి. ౨౦౪

వ్రాత వెంటగాని, వరమీ' డు దైవంబు,
చేత కొలది గాని, వ్రాత గాదు,
వ్రాతక' జుడు కర్త చేతకు దా కర్త. వి. ౨౦౫

దోసకారియైన, దూసరికాడై' న,
పగతుడై' న, వేద - బాహ్యుడై' న,
పట్టి లేని పేద వానికీ' దగునీ' వి,
ధనికునకు నొ' సంగ దగదు వేమ. ౨౦౬

---

203. He that fasts shall become *in his next birth* a village pig; he that embraces poverty shall become a beggar; and he that bows to a stone shall become like a lifeless image.

204. False is the creed of those who hold that it is profitable to renounce the present life: cannot ye see that eternal existence commences in this life.

205. The deity bestows on us that alone which is destined to us: what we gain is the result not of fate but our own conduct. Bramha is indeed the author of destiny, but we are the agents ourselves in all we do; *and shall be* rewarded or punished accordingly.

206. Be he an evil doer, or a reviler, spiteful, or unlearned,* if he is destitute it is fit to bestow alms on him: but what is the good of giving to those who already possess.

---

* Or anti-scriptural.

కంటి కంటిమ' నుచు, కర్మా' ధికారంబు,
వెంట బట్టి చెడును, వెర్రి జనుడు,
బట్ట బయిట ముక్తి బాటించి చూడరో! వి. ౨౦౭

తాను విమలుడై' క, తన గుణమ' ంతయు,
శివునికీ' ని గురువు, చెడుగు గురువు,
గుడ్డి గుర్రమె' క్కి, గుడి దిర్గిన' ట్లౌను. వి. ౨౦౮

జార-పురుషు మీద, సద్భక్తి సలుపుచు,
పతికిని చ్చకంబుఁ, బడయు భంగి,
పరము కొరకు యోగి, పాటించు దేహంబు. వి.

తనువు లోన జీవ-తత్వమె' రుంగక,
వేరె కలద' టంచు వెదుక నే' ల,
భానుడు' ండ, దివ్వెఁ బట్టి వెదుకు రీతి. వి. ౨౧౦

---

207. The fool says "I know, I have learned!" he slavishly follows the creed of works. He cannot see the truth when it is plainly revealed to him.

208. The teacher who has *in his own esteem* become pure, and yet has not devoted his entire heart to God, is the vilest of instructors: he is like him who should attempt to ride the ring on a blind horse.

209. Like as a woman who fixes her heart on a strange man, treats her husband with wheedling fondness; so does the devotee nourish his body—*not for its own sake, but* with a view to attaining the next world.

210. Ignorant that the living principle exists in your body, why do you search imagining that it is to be found elsewhere! ye are like one who, while the sun shines, should search with a lamp.

చదువుల'ందు లేదు; శాస్త్రంబులను లేదు;
వాదములను, దైవ-భేదములను,
బయిటను'న్న ముక్తి, బాటించ లేరయా. వి. ౨౧౧
చచ్చు వారిని గని, చావు నిశ్చయమ'ని,
తత్వమె'ల్లనా'త్మ దలచి తెలిసి,
నదరు, బెదరు, లేక, నడరిన ముక్తుడు. వి. ౨౧౨
బొమ్మలా'ట వాడు, బొమ్మలనా'డించు,
భువిని జనులు చూడ పొలుపు మీర,
తాను మరగియుండి, దైవమా'డించురా. వి. ౨౧౩
పర-యువతి రతంబు, పాటించి కోరితే;
కోటి పూజలె'ల్ల, కొల్ల బోవు,
సెగకు పొంత వెన్న, చెడదె తాపము చేత. వి.

---

211. It is not *to be found* by study; it is not in *royal* courts, neither in disputations nor in drawing distinctions in the divinity *according to discordant* creeds: ye cannot perceive the great object, though in itself evident.

212. He who sees that all men must die, and, knowing death is certain, fixes his soul in meditation on the divine essence; who is tree from fear and alarm, by the force of wisdom—this is the perfect man.

213. Just as a showman plays his puppets, while he lies hidden, so does the deity, while he conceals himself, admirably govern men.

214. If a man meditates adultery with the wife of his neighbour, when he gazes at her, all the fruits of his former good deeds, however numerous, shall melt away, as surely as butter in the heat of fire.

తప్పు రూపు గట్టి, ధరలోన దిరిగెడు,
సేతలె' ల్ల, మిత్తి జేరు విధము,
కడుపు నిండని' ంత, కష్టంబులే' లరా. వి. ౨౧౫

వాక్యశుద్ధి లేని వాడు, చండాలుండు,
ప్రేమ శుద్ధి లేక, పెట్టు టె' ల్లు,
నొసలు భక్తుడై' న, నోరు తోడేల' యా. వి. ౨౧౬

పరగ బ్రహ్మ - గుడ్డు * బరికించి చూచిన,
కులముల' న్ని' యందు గూడ బుట్టె
న' ందరొ' కట గలయున' న్న దమ్ములె కదా? వి.

కూడు' దే' మి జేసె, కులమే' మి చేసెను,
భూమి యేమి జేసె, బొందిక' ట్టె,
నరుడు బడెడు పాట్లు, నగు బాట్లు చూడగా. వి.

---

215. All acts that are performed † under a false guise are but *paths* leading to death: why is all this labour undergone to fill the belly?

216. He who is devoid of purity of speech is *no better than* a Pariar: to what end is liberality devoid of affection? he is in his forehead a worshipper, but in his mouth a wolf. ‡

217. If we carefully observe and examine the universe, we shall see that all castes equally originated therein: then all are equal; surely all men are brothers?

218. What matters food, or caste, or country, so as to affect our bodies? Surely the trouble men take *about caste* is all ridiculous!

---

* For బ్రహ్మాండం, the mundane egg.

† The word seta, answering to *pani*, work, is used colloquially instead of the gerund form.
So అట్లా చేసేపనికి వచ్చినాడు is the same as చేసినందుకు.

‡ See verse 193 and note.

కానలేరు గాని, కలి - యుగంబునను' న్న,
మనుజుల' ందరికిని, మాన మొ' కటి,
దాష్టికుల' గు వారు, తమవలె జూడక,
పరుల బోవనా' డుదురు ర వేమ. ౨౧౯

జాతుల' ందు నె' ట్టి జాతి ముఖ్యము చూడ,
మెరుక లేక దిరుగనే' మి గలదు,
మెరుక గలుగు మనుజుడే' జాతి గలవాడు. వి. ౨౨౦

చావు వచ్చిన' ప్పుడు, సన్యసించేదె' ట్లు,
కడకు మొదటి కులము జెడిన యట్లు,
పాపమొ' కటి గలదు, ఫలమే' మి లేద' యా! వి.

ఊరులు, పల్లెలు, మానుక,
వారక యడవిం జరించి, వాడ' (రుద' ంచుక, *)
వేరులు, గూరలు, మెస వెడు,
వీరడికె' † ట మోక్ష - పదవి? వినరా వేమా. ౨౨౨

---

219. They cannot perceive in this iron age that the respectability of all men *in regard of caste* is the same. The blustering fool looks upon no one as his equal, and scorns all men.

220. Consider; is any one caste superior to the rest? what is the use of living without understanding? the man of understanding may be born in any tribe whatever.

221. What is the profit of turning religious at the time of death, as if your former state were thereby altered? your sins remain unchanged and you are none the better.

222. He leaves the towns and villages, and unweariedly roams the wilds, as though this were any extraordinary merit; how shall the simpleton who feeds on roots and herbs attain to the abode of bliss?

---

*Al. జరించి, వాగరుడ,ంచుక. † Al. వీరడికట.

శూద్రులనుచు భువిని, శూద్రుల బోనాడు
మాలకన్న చెడుగు మహిని లేడు,
నరకమునకునేగు నష్టమైన వెనుక. వి. ౨౨౩

పూజకన్న నెంచ, బుద్ధి నిదానంబు,
మాటకన్న నెంచ మనసు దృఢము;
కులముకన్న మిగుల గుణమె ప్రధానంబు. వి. ౨౨౪

కులము హెచ్చు తగ్గు, కొదవలు పని లేదు,
సాను జాతమయ్యె, సకల కులము,
హెచ్చు తగ్గుమాట లెట్లెరుంగగ వచ్చు? వి.

గ్రామము, భూములు, మానుక,
ప్రేమయు దయ యింత లేక, భీకర-మతులై,
భామల, సుతులను, వదలుక,
బాముల బడనేల, యడవి పట్టున, వేమా. ౨౨౬

---

223. There is not a viler wretch in the earth than him who scorns other men, calling them Sudras : after his death he shall fall into hell.

224. Wisdom is a surer reliance than empty worship : the mind is more to be depended on than mere words ; and a man's virtues are of more importance than his caste.

225. Disputations as to which caste is the best are all fruitless : all the tribes originated in the same origin : who can decide as to the superiority or inferiority of any one.

226. They desert their own town and land, and, devoid of the smallest love and affection, with repulsive manners, they leave both wives and sons, to suffer misery—and to what end is it?

మాలవానినేల, మహిమీఁద నిందింప
నొడల రక్తమాంసమొకటి గాదె?
వాని లోన మెలఁగు వాని కులంబేది? వి. ౨౨౭
మాల-వానినంటి, మరి నీళ్ల మునిఁగేరు,
మనుజ-కర్మ * చేత మాలఁడయ్యె,
నేల దెలియలేరొ యీ నర-పశువులు. వి. ౨౨౮
మాదిగ యన వద్దు, మరి గుణ మొనఁగిన,
మాదిగని వసిష్ఠు, మగువ దేడె, †
మాదిగ గుణమున్న మరి ద్విజుఁడగునయా? వి.
శిలను ప్రతిమ జేసి చీకటింటను బెట్టి,
మ్రొక్క పలదు, వెర్రి మూఢులార!
యుల్లమందు బ్రహ్మ యుండుట దెలియరు. వి. ౨౩౦

---

227. Why should we constantly revile the Pariar? are not his flesh and blood the same as our own? and of what caste is He who pervades the Pariar *as well as all other men*?

228. Why should you plunge in water *to purify yourself* if a Pariar touches you? He became what he is in consequence of his sins in a former birth: *how stupid are those* who cannot comprehend this?

229. Call not him an outcast who possesses a good disposition. Did not *the hermit* Vasishta take a Pariar wife? how can he be called a Brahmin whose qualities are those of a Pariar?

230. O make not a stone image, to be put in a dark chamber and worshipped! Oh ignorant creatures, know ye not that the deity dwells in the heart alone!

---

* Al· మాలకర్మములన.   † తేడు for తేయుడు.

మాలవాఁడ' యినను మరియా' త్మ మీఁదను,
మనసు నిల్పెనే' ని మాల గాఁడు
మనసు నిల్పకు' న్న, మహి మీఁద మాలఁడు. వి.

తాత గన్న తల్లి, తమ తండ్రి గను తల్లి,
తన్ను గన్న తల్లి, తల్లి తల్లి, *
తల్లి శూద్రురాలు, తా నె, ట్లు బాపఁడో. వి. ౨౩౨

తాత జనించె కన్యకకు,
తండ్రులు తాము ను కుండ గోళకుల్
మాత పరానుకూలి, [మరి
మక్కువ] ద్రౌపది భర్తలే' వురుఁ,
నీతుల జెప్ప, పాండవుల
నీమములి' ట్టివి, ? యంచు నె' న్నుచుఁ,
భూతలమ' ందు మిక్కిలిగ
బూమెల జేసిరి! వెర్రి వేమనా. ౨౩౩

231. Though a man be by birth an outcast, if he orders his heart aright he is no outcast : he who cannot govern his affections is the vilest of the vile.

232. If your grandfather's mother, and your father's mother, your own mother, and your mother's mother, be a Sudra woman, how can you be a Bramin.

233. Their grandsire was born of an unmarried
n, their fathers and they themselves were the illegiti-
children of a wife and a widow. Their mother was a
of strange men, and then her five husbands! If you
their morals, such were the practices of the Pandavas.
falsehoods are the greatest in the world !†

---

se are allusions to the incidents related in the Mahabharata, the India (to use Sir Wm. Jones' expression), wherein the deeds of

తల్లి - తల్లి - తల్లి - తల్లి - తల్లి.

P. T. O.

తనదు తల్లి లంజె, తన యాలు మాదిగె,
శ్రీ పతికి గురువు వసిష్ఠుఁడ' రయ
తపము చేత ద్విజుఁడు! తర్కింప కులమె' ట్లు? వి.
జాతి వేరు లేక, జన్మ - క్రమంబున,
నెమ్మదిని నభవుని, నిల్పునే' ని,
యఖిల జనులకె' ల్లనా' తఁడు ఘనుఁడయా. వి. ౨౩౫

234. His mother was a prostitute, and his wife a Pariar yet Vasishtha * was the tutor to the noble Rama: by austerities he became a Bramin, but if you look to his caste, what is it like?

235. He is the truly excellent man, and superior to all the sects, who draws no invidious distinctions between the castes: by practising the rites ordained for his tribe he will fix the deity in his heart.

---

the Pandavas are described. The *grandsire* is Vyasa, whom Yojanagandhi bore to Parasara: the Pandavas were born of Cunti Devi and of Madri, wives to king Pandu; the "mother" is a term equally applied to these wives: and Draupadi was the wife by turns of the five sons of Pandu: who were Dharmaraz, Bhima, Arjuna, Nacula, and Sahadeva, the three first being sons of Cunti Devi and the last two the offspring of Madri. The last couplet sometimes appears thus, with a defective rhyme.

జ్ఞాతుల జంపు పాతకులు,
పాండవులే' వురు సత్యుల' ంచుదా,
భూతలమె' ల్ల మెచ్చిక్కఁగను,
పుణ్యులు లేదురు బొంక వేమనా.

*Urvasi, the courtezan, was his mother; Arundhati his wife.

ధర గిరులు జలధుల న్నియు,
పరికింపగ ప్రళయమునను, భస్మా - కృతులౌ
సురలును మునులును జనగా,
నెర యోధులును ండ గలరె నేర్పున వేమా? ౨౩౬
ఉర్వి వారికెల్ల నొక్క-కంచము బెట్టి,
పొత్తు గుడిపి కులము, పొలియ జేసి,
తలను చెయ్యి బెట్టి, తగ నమ్మ జెప్పరా? వి. ౨౩౭
గట్టురాళ్ల దెచ్చి, కాళ్ల చేతుల ద్రొక్కి-,
కాసె - యులుల చేత, గాసి జేసి,
మొరప - రాళ్ల కెరగు, మొప్పెలనే' మందు! వి.
తోలు - కడుపులోన, దొడ్డ వాడు'ండగ,
రాతి గుళ్లలోన, రాశి బోయ,
రాళ్లు దేవుడై'న, రాసులు మింగవా? వి. ౨౩౯

---

236. This earth, with its mountains and seas, shall in the final destruction be all consumed: then shall the gods and the prophets perish, and how shall even the victorious survive?*

237. Place one dish before all the men in the world and let them eat together, abolishing their castes: lay thy hand on their heads, and convince them *that their present distinctions are absurd.*

238. What can we think of the fools who bring mountainstones *together*, knock them about with their hands and feet, and after tormenting them with mason's chisels, bow down to the rugged blocks?

239. While he who is *alone* honourable dwells with your own fleshly bodies, † why should ye heap up *offerings* in temples made of stone. How can gods made of stone feed on those heaps?

---

* Or, Then shall only the spotless live.

† Lit. in the belly of the skin, that is, within the skin.

రాతి బసవని గని, రంగుగా మ్రొక్కుచు,
గునుక * బసవని గని, గుద్దుచు' ండ్రు;
బసవ భక్తులె' ల్ల పాపులు తలపోయ. † వి. ౨౪౦
మన్ను మెత్తి కరిగి, మరి రూపు గావించి,
గుంట నిండ బూడ్చి, గురుతు నిల్పి,
మనుజులె' ల్ల గూడి, మరి దేవుడ' ందురు. వి. ౨౪౧
మంచి శకునముల' ని, మెంచి పెండిలి యాడ,
వారలొ' కరు లేరు, వసుధలోన; †
జనుల కర్మములను, శకునముల్ నిల్పునా? వి.
గూబ యెక్కిన' ట్టి, గురము † పాడుగ బెట్టి,
వెళ్లి పోదుర' ంత వెర్రివారు
గూబ యేమి చేసె, గురమే' మి చేయును? వి.

---

240. If you see a bull made of marble, you bow down ceremoniously to it; but if you see a trotting bullock you *do not scruple to* beat it; surely the worshippers of the bull are wretched sinners!

241. You apply clay *over the waxen mould*, melt it, and form a certain figure: fill the hollow *with melted metal*, and set up *the statue* as a sign; then people assemble and call this a god!

242. Of all those who looked well for good omens at their marriage, has even one survived *free from the common fate of mortals*? Not one! men depend on their conduct alone: can any omens render them stable?

243. They leave a house desolate if an owl perches upon it: they flee as if mad: what mischief has the owl done? what fault is there in the house?

---

* Al. గుండుబసువ † Al. పశువు లెమరి యేమి
‡ Al. వరసి చూడ which gives an incorrect rhyme.
See notes on II., 177 and 192.

విష - సహితులు నరులు, విష - ధరులెన్నఁగ,
వృషభ వృషణములను, విరియఁ గొట్ట,
నఘము వచ్చు కడకునాయువు గొదువఁగు. వి.

వేముఁ పాలు బోసి, వెయ్యేండ్లు పెంచిన,
చేదు విడిచి తీపి, జెందనటుల
నోఁగు గుణము విడిచి, యుచితజ్ఞుఁడగునెట్లు? వి.

వాడ వదిన కేల, వాని వర్తనములు?
చాడి గానికేల, జాడ బుద్ధి?
మూఢ మతులకేల, ముదమఃతో జ్ఞానంబు. వి.

నేరనన్న వాడు, నెర జాణ మహిలోన,
నేర్తునన్న వాడు, వార్త - కాడు;
యూరకున్న వాడె యుత్తమోత్తముఁడెందు. వి.

---

244. How wicked are the *cruel who venture to geld oxen*: they will certainly meet with retribution.

245. Though you were to nourish a margosa tree with milk for a thousand years, will it lose its bitterness and become sweet? Never will the sinner change his nature, however instructed.

246. What can the prostitute know of the feelings of consanguinity? or the talebearer, of propriety and sense? or the stupid fool, of discretion?

247. He who says, "I know nothing," is the shrewdest of all: he who says, "I am learning," is a mere talker. He who holds his peace is the wisest and the best.

దూలా' లు కొంకిను' ండిన,
వాలాయము చేటు వచ్చు, వసుమతి లోనఁ,
లోలాక్షి విడిచి పెట్టిన,
మేలిమి గా బ్రతుక వచ్చు, మేదిని వేమా. ౨౪౮

మానినీ మనోజ-మందిరా' నందై ' క
లోలుడో' ల్లదూ' ర్ధ్వ లోక సుఖము
మాల వాడ కుక్క, మరియు' న్న మె' రుగునా. వి.

తొత్తు తొత్తె కాని, దొర-సాని గాబోదు
హత్తదె' పుడు, దానికై' న గుణము,
మిత్తికూళ్ల దొంగ, మేలె' ర్గ నేర్చునా. వి. ౨౫౦

నాణ్యమై' న చెడిపె, * నయమె' రిగి మెలంగు;
విటుని కు స్తరించు, వివరమె, రుగు;
బానిసై' న తొత్తు, పాటించ రాదయా. వి. ౨౫౧

---

248. He who *forms vile connections* will certainly suffer for them ; forsake them and live at ease.

249. He who is *devoted to sesnual pleasures* shall never know the joys of the next world. Can the dog reared by a Pariar have any better food ? †

250. She who is *low by nature* can never be made a lady ; no good quality can ever attach to her : will one who lives by stealing beggar's morsels ever get anything better ?

251. An elegant courtezan will conduct herself with civility : she caresses her lover, and is prudent : but who pays any attention to a vulgar slut ?

---

* Al. లంజ.

† The expressions used in this and a few other verses are such as cannot with propriety be translated into English. Some epigrams are wholly omitted as objectionable.

పందన ధికు జేసి, ఁబవరంబునకు ఁబంప,
పారి - పోవు కార్య భంగమ' వును
పారు వాడు బంటు పనికి రాడ' ందును. వి. ౨౫౨

తిరుమలకును ఁబోవ, తురక దాసరి ఁగాడు,
కాశి ఁబోవ, లంజె గరిత గాదు,
కుక్క సింహమ' గునె, గోదావరికి ఁబోవ. వి. ౨౫౩

కులుకు గుబ్బ ఁజూపి, గొబ్బున గరగించి,
చేతి కాసు లె' ల్ల, చేర దీయు
న' తను చేతి కత్తుల' మరంగ కాంతలు. వి. ౨౫౪

అనుకూల్యము గల యంగన గలిగిన,
సతికి పతికి పరమ - సౌఖ్యమ' మరు,
ప్రాతికూల్యమై' న, పరిహరింప సుఖంబు. వి. ౨౫౫

---

252. If a coward is made a general and sent to battle, he will fly, and all will be ruined : of what avail is a soldier who flees the enemy ?

253. Though a Turk go to the sacred hill *of Tripety*, he does not become a palmer ; going on *pilgrimage* to Benares will not make a modest woman of a prostitute : though a dog go *to the sacred stream of* the Godaveri, will it make him a lion ?

254. At the sight of her charms you are melted *with love*, and the courtezan strips you of every farthing. Surely lovely women are the darts in the hand of Cupid.

255. If the wife be agreeable to her husband, this forms the sweetest happiness to the married pair. But if she be disagreeable, the only happiness is in quitting her.

గొప్ప పిరుదు గన్న, *కుచ-కుంభముల గన్న
చెప్ప రాని చోట చేవ † గన్న
ముప్పిరి-గొనున' య్యా మొనసిన మోహంబు. ‡ వి.

"కాశి! కాశి!" యనుచు, కడు వేడ్కతో బోదు
ర' ందు గలుగు దేవుడి' ందు లేడ?
యిందున' ందు గలడు, హృదయంబు లెస్సై' న. వి.

---

256. If he sees plump limbs, a fair breast, *and other charms,* surely three-fold love § will enter, and quell even a hermit.

257. "Benares ! Benares !" cry they, and delight to travel there : yet is not same God here as there ? If thy heart be right he is there and here also.

---

*Al. కొప్పుచెలువుగన్న or కొప్పుబిరుదుకన్న.

† Al. కోటుచెలవు, or సెలవు, *i. e.*, the corner of the mouth ; also, a pit in a rock. Al. చెలిమి agreeableness, affection, gracefulness : చేవ plumpness is perhaps the true reading.

‡ Al. మునికైన మోహంబు.

§ *Mup-piri* ; perhap from ముప్పురి (from పురి a thread or stand in a cord), and *mu* for *mudu*, three. It is commonly applied in the poets to strong passion : so.

ఉ. ముప్పిరి కొన్న వేడ్కసర
మోహినిపై నెలకొన్న,

Vicramarca Charitra, v., 191.

క. నొప్పించి, పెద్ద కోపము
ముప్పురి కొన, నాగ పాశముల బంధించెన్.

Vishnu Purana, VIII., 188.

మతము దారి మరచు, మధురా' ధరము జూచి,
మగువ రూపు జూచి, మనసు మరచు,
యోని జూచి, సర్వ యోగంబు మరచు, రా. వి.

నీళ్ల మునుగనే' ల? నిధుల మెట్టగనే' ల?
మొనసి వేల్పులకును మ్రొక్కనే' ల?
కపట - కల్మషములు కడుపులో నుం' డగా. వి. ౨౫౯

కూడు చీర బాసి, గుళ్ల పంచల బడు
న' ట్లు వ్రాసె బ్రహ్మ యతుల నుదుట,
తోయజా - క్షి జేర, దోషంబుల' ంటునా? వి.

కుంటి కుక్క కే' ల, కుందేటి పరువులు?
పిరికి బంటు కే' ల, బిరుదు గొడుగు?
ముసలి ముండ కే' ల, ముసి ముసి నగవులు? వి.

---

258. Gazing at a sweet lip he forgets the path of religion: when he sees a woman's face he forgets himself. * * *

259. To what end is it that you plunge in the holy waters? Why go and touch sacred places? Why attempt to worship the deity while your bellies are full of foul hypocrisy?

260. To give up food and apparel, and lie about in the porches of temples, is the fate written *for their sins* in the foreheads of monks: what would they be the worse for familiarity with women?

261. Can a lame dog equal the swiftness of the hare What has a cowardly soldier to do with *honorabl* insignia and the *golden* umbrella. * * *

ఎంత భూమి దిరిగి, యే పాటు బడుచున్న
నంటనీ కప్రాప్తి వెంట దిరుగు;
భూమి క్రొత్తమైన, భోక్తలు క్రొత్తలా? వి.

పరగ జలకమాడి, పట్టె నామము దీర్చి,
నీరు-కావి పంచె, నెరయ గట్టి,
వారి-కాంత జూచి, వ్రతమెల్ల మరుచు రా. వి.

మనసు నిల్ప లేని మాయ-విరక్తులు,
మనసు పడుచురొక్క మగువ మీద
యిట్టి వ్యర్థ జన్మమీ బ్రతుకేటికి? వి. ౨౬౪

తొడల మెరుపు జూచి, తోరంపు కుచములు, *
వార కొప్పు గలుగు వనిత జూచి, †
విటుడు నిలుచునెట్లు, విరహాగ్ని జొరకను? వి.

---

262. Wherever you roam, whatever toils you undergo: your fate is *unalterable and* still follows you: though the land, *you wander in* be new to you, you remain the same.

263. After *religiously* bathing, and drawing the line and streak in his forehead, and trimly putting on a tinted vest should he chance to see a courtezan, he forgets all his vows!

264. Those false ascetics who are unable to stay their heart, let their thoughts dwell on a woman: how unprofitable is their life! to what end were they born?

265. When he beholds the beauty of her form, and her flowing tresses, how can the lover abstain from loving a beauteous woman?

* Al. వొప్పు చన్నులు జూచి. † Al. వనిత సొగసు కొండె వంక జూచి.

కాశి నీళ్లు మోసి, కాళ్లు మొగము వాచి,
యొందు సుఖము లేకనెండి యెండి,
చచ్చి, వెనుక ముక్తి, సాధింప గలరెకో? వి.
దేశ దేశములను, గాసిలి, తిరుగంగ
నాత్మయందు ధ్యానమంటుకొనునె?
కాసులకును దిరుగ, కలుగునా మోక్షంబు? వి.
కచ్చుమీది యాస, కనకంబు పై యాస
లేని వాడు, పుడమి లేని వాడు;
గలిగనేని, యతడు గానంగ రాడయా. వి. ౨౬౮
వలపు దీరెనేని, వనజాక్షి యధరంబు
ములక-పంటి గిజరు, ముష్టి రసము,
చింత లేని వేళ, జీవ-సమానమో * వి. ౨౬౯

---

266. Though you bear about the sacred water of Benares and your feet and faces swell with the heat of travel, devoid of repose, how shall you after death attain heaven *by such means* !†

267. Though you roam from land to land, how can this fix religion in your heart? how can travelling about for the sake of alms gain you heaven?

268. He who has no desire *of women* or of riches, is nowhere to be found in the earth: should there be such a one, his virtue would yet be unknown to men.

269. When love is over, the cherry lip of the rosy girl is tasteless as the pulp of the night-shade berry, or the juice of the poison-nut. When you do not care for it, it is as disgusting as the milk *of the mango leaf.*

---

* Al. చింత-పండు రసము జీడి రసము బోలు.

† Alluding to the men who carry water drawn in the Ganges to Rameswaram, where they pour it over the idol.

చదువులెల్ల జదివి, సర్వజ్ఞుడై యుండి, *
బ్రహ్మ విద్యలెల్ల, పదట గలిపి,
యిరుకు యోనిఁజూచి, పరమయోగము మాను. † వి.

తాను నిలుచు చోట, దైవము లేదని,
పామర జనుఁడు తిరుపతుల దిగిరి,
జోము వీడి చేతి సొమ్మెల్లఁ బోఁ-జేసి,
చెడి గృహంబు తానుఁజేరు వేమ. ౨౭౧

కాశి, మధుర, కాంచి, గయ, ప్రయాగయు, సేతు
వాస తోడ వీటినాత్మఁజూచి,
వాసనను దెలియుడు, వట్టి వెట్టి విధంబు. వి. ౨౭౨

---

270. After going through all his studies, and attaining consummate wisdom, after making nothing of divinity, *the moment* he sees *a fair woman* he forgets all his sanctity.

271. Fools roam to holy places imagining that the deity is not to be found where they dwell: they merely exercise their limbs ‡ and squander their money; they are ruined, and so return home!

272. Casi, Madura, Conjeveram, Gaya, Prayag, Setu; though a man visit all these holy places with an ardent mind, what benefit does he derive? this is mere drudgery! §

---

* సర్వ &c. Al. చాల వివేకియై.

† Al. యోనిచూచి, పొంగి యోగంబు మరుచును.

‡ Lit. Get rid of the cramp, or torpidity in the limbs.

§ A great number of verses appear in various manuscripts, exhibiting the same sentiment in various forms; a few alone have been inserted in the present chapter as amply sufficient.

చదువు జదువనే' ల, సన్యాసి గానే' ల,
షణ్మతముల జిక్కి చావనే' ల;
యతని భజన జేసి, యాత్మలో దెలియుడీ. వి.

మనము లోన బుట్టు, మరి కోర్కె లె' న్నియు;
కోర్కె లె' ందు ముక్తి కుదుగు పడదు;
మనము బ్రహ్మమె' నుచు, మది నె' రుంగగ లేరు. వి.

చదువు లె' న్ని జదివి, చాల వివేకింప,
కపటికె' న్ననే' ల, కలుగు ముక్తి?
దాలి - గుంట కుక్క దలచిన చందము. వి. ౨౭౫

తరుచు చదువు చదువ, తర్క వాదమె కాని,
దివ్య జ్ఞానమునకు తేట పడదు;
పసిరి* కాయ పురుగు పగిదిని చెడిపోవు. వి. ౨౭౬

---

273. To what end is all 'this reading ? what is the fruit of a monkish life ? why perish entangled in the six *conflicting* creeds ? worship Him, and know Him who dwells in your heart †

274. All our passions originate in the heart : but emancipation from sin is inconsistent with these desires : can ye not see that the soul is one with the divinity ?

275. Though he have read all that can be read, and be an acute disputant, never shall the hypocrite attain to final happiness. His meditations are like those of the dog on the dunghill ‡

276. Excessive study leads only to disputatious talking : a man does not hereby attain divine knowledge : he is *entangled therein* like a silk-worm in its shell.

* This word is often erroneously spelt పిసినికాయ

† The six doctrines denominated Pashanda, Bauddha, Charvaca, Saiva, Ganesa, and Vaishnava.

‡ In real misery, though apparently at ease. This verse appears in several different forms.

అవును వేమన్న జెప్పిన యాత్మ బుద్ధి
తెలియ లేన ట్టి యజ్ఞాని దేబెలకును
తలకు బాసిన వెంట్రుక వలెను జూడ
భుక్తి ముక్తులు హీనమై పోవు వేమ. ౨౭౭

ఇట్టి సాధు-విద్య యెంత లేద' ని చూచి,
గాధ-విద్య నేర్చి కాన లేక,
సాధు సజ్జనముల సాంగత్యమె' రుగక,
బాధ పడుదురు తుద, పరులు వేమ. ౨౭౮

ఇదియు పరమ' ట' ంచుని' తర-చింతల విడి,
మనసు జెదర నీక, మట్టు పెట్టి,
కొదువ లేక నిలువ, కోర్కులు ఫలియించు,
మనసు లోనను' ండు మహిమ వేమ. ౨౭౯

---

277. Verily the foolish wretches, who are unable to comprehend the mental wisdom taught by Vemana, shall perish like a hair when separated from the head, devoid of sustenance here and perfection hereinafter.

278. Those who look upon this excellent knowledge with scorn, and learn only abstruse sciences, shall not attain to it; they shall never know the society of the good and wise, but shall, as strangers *to virtue*, ultimately fall into misery.

279. And he who holds this superexcellent, who gives up all other cares, who lets not his mind wander, but restrains it, he shall stand fast without fail, all his wishes shall be accomplished and his soul shall be full of glory.

THE END

INDEX TO INITIAL WORDS OF THE EPIGRAMS.

For Copies Apply to :—

V. RAMASWAMY SASTRULU & SONS,

192, Esplanade, } MADRAS.
323, Tondiarpet. }

		ప్రతి 1-కి రూ.	అ.
ఆంధ్రనామసంగ్రహము, పద్యవ్యాఖ్యానము, మూలము	...	0	3
,, టీకతో (గ్లేజు పేపరు)	...	0	8
ఆంధ్రనామసంగ్రహము, ఆంధ్రనామశేషము, సాంబనిఘంటువు కాలికో	...	2	0
ఆంధ్రభాషాభూషణము, విమర్శతో	...	0	6
ఆంధ్రశ్రీమద్రామాయణము—జనమంచి శేషాద్రిశర్మగారిది, 3 సంపుటములు	...	15	0
డిటో 7 సంపుటములు	...	18	0
ఆంధ్రభాషార్ణవము	...	1	0
ఉత్తరరామాయణము, చక్కనిమాప్ప	..	6	0
ఉత్తరహరివంశము	..	3	0
కవిరాజమనోరంజనము	..	1	4
కృష్ణదండకము	..	0	2
కృష్ణరాయవిజయము	..	0	8
కాశీఖండము	...	3	8
కుచేలోపాఖ్యానము, సటీక, (భాగవతము	...	0	6
డిటో గట్టుప్రభుకృతము	...	0	8
కుమారసంభవము, నన్నెచోడకృతము	...	5	0
గజేంద్రమోక్షము. సటీక	...	0	10
గదోపాఖ్యానము, రామనామాత్యునిది	...	0	12
గద్యపద్యసంగ్రహము, విద్వాన్ జ. వే. సుబ్రహ్మణ్యశర్మగారిది		0	8
,, గొర్తి సూర్యనారాయణశాస్త్రిగారిది	...	0	12
గరుడాచలము-యక్షగానము, పెద్దమ్మ	...	0	3
గీతమంజరి, చిలకమర్తి లక్ష్మీనరసింహము	...	0	4
చిత్రభారతము, చరిగొండ ధర్మనగారిది	...	1	8
చెన్నపురీవిలాసము	...	0	8
చెన్నబసవపురాణము	...	1	0
ఛందోదర్పణము (అనంతునిఛందము)	...	2	0

		ప్రతి 1-కి రూ
శకునసమస్యలు	...	1
దశావతారచరిత్ర	...	3
దసరాపద్యములు	...	0
దేశింగురాజుకథ (జంగంకథ)	...	0
ధ్రువోపాఖ్యానము, సటీక	...	0
నలోపాఖ్యానము, సటీక	..	
నలచరిత్ర, ద్విపద, ప్యాలిస్ సైజు	...	
నిర్వచనోత్తరరామాయణము	...	
నిరంకుశోపాఖ్యానము	...	
నీతిపద్యసంగ్రహము, సటిప్పణము	...	0
నీలాసుందరీపరిణయము	...	0
పంచతంత్రము, నారాయణకవిది	...	1
డిటో కాలికో సైజు	...	2
డిటో వేంకటనాథ రాజకవికృతము	...	1
డిటో గాలికో సైజు	...	2
పల్నాటివీరచరిత్రము	...	3
ప్రభావతీప్రద్యుమ్నము	..	1
పారిజాతాపహరణము, చిన్నసైజు	...	1
,, టీకాతాత్పర్యసహితము	...	3
బ్రహ్మోత్తరఖండము, క్రొత్తకూర్పు	..	1
మనుచరిత్ర, సటీక, వావిళ్ల రామస్వామిశాస్త్రిగారి వ్యాఖ్యానముతో చిన్నసైజున మేలుకాగితములమీద ముద్రితము	...	5
మహాశ్విముప్పట, వే. ప్రభాకరశాస్త్రి	...	0
మార్కండేయపురాణము	...	3
మొల్లరామాయణము (న్యూసుపేపరు)	...	1
యయాతిచరిత్ర, పొన్నిగంటి తెలగనార్య	...	1

వావిళ్ల రామస్వామిశాస్త్రులు అండ్ సన్స్
292, ఎస్ప్లనేడ్, మ